Songs 'Round The Campfire

Songs by "Hi" Busse, Tom Chambers,

Robert Meyer, Dan Meyer, Tom Spaulding,

Bob Wagoner, Buck Page, John Ryberg,

John Lamont, Carson Robinson, and Tex Ritter

T0087319

Compiled by Ron Middlebrook

Special thanks to:
Gregory Hermon, R. C. Allen,
Greg Scott, Rick Huff,
Howard Wright

Cover Art by Eddie Young
Transcribing & Typesetting Dereck Cornett

Despite an exhaustive search, we have been unable to locate the publishers or copyright owners of some of the songs in this book. Therefore, we have proceeded on the assumption that no formal copyright claims have been filed on these works. If we have inadvertently published apreviously copyrighted composition without permission, we advise the copyright owner(s) to contact us so that we may give credit in future editions.

ISBN 0-931759-86-2
SAN 683-8022

Copyright © 1994 CENTERSTREAM Publishing
P.O. Box 17878 – Anaheim CA 92817

All rights for publication and distribution are reserved. No part of this book may be reproduced in any form or by any electronic or mechanical means including information storage and retrieval systems without permission in writing from the publisher, except by reviewers who may quote brief passages in review.

CONTENTS

Features

"We had a splendid campfire that night. After supper and the first guard had taken the herd, smoking and story tellin' was the order of the evening. The campfire is to all outdoor life what the evening fireside is to domestic life after the labors of the day are over, the men gather round the fire and the social hour is spend yarning."

Andy Adams
Cowboy

Mess wagon on timber creek at night, c. 1938
Buffalo Bill Historical Center, Cody, WY Charles Belden Photograph Collection

"HI" BUSSE
& THE FRONTIERSMEN

Born in Warroad, Minnesota in 1914, "Hi" Busse is the sole surviving member of Jack Dalton's original Riders Of The Purple Sage . . .the KFI Radio touring group from 1934 that was the first to use the name. It was Dalton who told the tall young accordionist he had hired . . . Enright August Busse . . . that a name like that would "never do" and gave him the handle "High Pockets", later shortened to "Hi". The Riders' custom radio theme ARIZONA HERE I COME, with other lyrics, later became Rex Allen's hit MY DEAR OLD ARIZONA HOME.

"Hi" Busse
<u>**1993 Western Music Association Hall of Fame photo**</u>

After a stint with The Texas Ramblers, "Hi" provided accordion support for Rex's uncle "Cactus Mack" (MacPeters) & The Saddletramps in a series of radio transcriptions, and also headlined with them them at the 1936 Texas Centinnial . . . breaking all Gulf Studio attendance records.

"Hi" founded The Frontiersmen, known later also as the Frontiersmen & Joanie (Hall), and The Frontiersmen Family, in 1938 . . . making it the second oldest western band, and the only group from Western Music's Golden Age to still boast a founding member. Other prominent former members include Rusty Richards, Wayne West and Eddie Martin, creator of the 3-Bank Steel Guitar with tone changers (a Frontiersmen "first"!)

"Hi" made westerns with Buck Jones, Smith Ballew, Charles Starrett, and toured with cowboy stars Tom Keene and Wesley Tuttle. With Roy Rogers, The Frontiersmen premiered the songs DUST (1938, Capitol Theater, Dallas, at Roy's first appearance using the name), ALONG THE NAVAJO TRAIL and DON'T FENCE ME IN (1945, Madison Square Garden). They were the first group to record with Ray Price when he turned to C&W. With Eddie Dean, The Frontiersmen recorded the first hit versions of ONE HAS MY NAME (1947) and HILLBILLY HEAVEN (1955), the latter written by then-Frontiersmen bandmember Hal Southern. They became the first western group ever to record THE WAYWARD WIND. With Rex Allen Jr., they premiered CAN YOU HEAR THOSE PIONEERS (1973 Phoenix, Arizona). And then, on the occasion of his WMA

Hall Of Fame induction, "Hi" Busse & The Frontiersmen proudly premiered their recording of the great Curley Fletcher's "newly-discovered" song THERE'S A ROUND-UP OUT IN RANGELAND TODAY! "Hi" was inducted into The Western Music Hall Of Fame at the Western Music Festival held November 1993 in Tucson Arizona.

"Hi" Busse was co-creator and participant in two popular comedy acts--The Simp-Phoneys, which arranged the classics for bottles & pans, and the hillbilly knockabout troupe Three Shifless Skonks.

Other career highlights include stints with western bandleader Happy Perryman, being the houseband for Squeakin' Deacon Moore's classic west coast radio program (backing Johnny Horton and The Mandrell Sisters among others), and 2 1/2 years on the early color telecast Doye O'Dell's Western Varieties. But their willingness to tour and reputation for professionalism made "Hi" Busse & The Frontiersmen one of the most sought-after western backup bands in the business . . . resulting in tours with Tex Ritter, Rex Allen, Roy Rogers and Dale Evans, Buddy Ebsen, Tex Williams, The Bonanza Cast, The Gunsmoke Cast including Kitty, Doc & Festus, Dale Robertson, High O"Brien, Ray Whitley & more. ("Hi" also hooked The Reinsmen up with Rex Allen and by cutting a special 78 RPM record for Roy Rogers to hear featuring The Frontiersmen backing Tommy Doss in a perfect impression of Bob Nolan & The Sons Of The Pioneers, directly enabled Doss to replace Nolan as the Pioneers' lead vocalist in the late 1940's).

In 1986, with writer/producer Rick Huff, "Hi" co-created the western music radio series SONG & STORY, on which he serves as "host". 1991 saw his life and career chronicled in a program for distribution by PBS, and in 1992 he hosted the feature video Ghosts Of New Mexico.

As time and opportunity allow, "Hi" Busse and today's version of The Frontiersmen still perform the great western music he loves!

A campfire shot of Jack Dalton's "Riders Of The Purple Sage",
Hi is kneeling down by the campfire. The car license says 1933

5

"Cactus Mack" and his Saddle Tramps
from left, Bob Fite,
"Cactus Mack" MacPeters,
"Stepladder" Fite,
Hi Pockets, and Jimmy Carol
Cactus Mack was the
uncle of Rex Allen. c. 1935,

A photo still from the film "The Medico of Painted Springs," Hi with the squeeze box as part of his comedy troupe "The Simp-Phoneys". c.1941

Newspaper advertising for the movie "The Medico of Painted Springs"

Publicity shot for Hi
with the Simp-Phonies, c. 1941

Hi and the boys
with guitar great
Merle Travis

I'm Just A Tumbleweed

Words and Music by:
Eddie Martin and Hi Busse

Brightly

I'M JUST A TUM - BLE - WEED a roll - in' o'er the prai - rie, Ain't got no friends, no home, no place to go, I'll (just) keep right on a-roll - in' o'er the prai - rie, Till I find a place that I can call my own. I hear the wind a-blow - in' o'er the prai - rie, It's tak - in' me where I don't want to go, JUST A TUM - BLE - WEED a roll - in' 'cross the prai - rie and I'll al - ways have to fol - low it, I know. Git a - long, lit - tle po - ny, git a - long, don't you tar - ry on your way _____ Git a -

© 1948 "Hi" Busse and Eddie Martin
Used by Permission

long, lit - tle po - ny, ('cause) we ain't got time to stay. _____

_____ I've been a drift - in' ev - er since my child - hood, But

now I'm head - in' for the Great Di - vide, JUST A TUM - BLE - WEED a roll - in' o'er the

1.
prai - rie, As I jog a - long I'll bid the world good - bye, JUST A

2.
jog a - long I'll bid the world good - bye.

"Hi" with Roy Rogers on tour 1945

Ridin' The Range

This tune was used on the Frontiersmen's 1949 radio broadcast transcriptions, and became a set-opener for the group.

Words and Music by:
E. A. "Hi" Busse

© 1948 E. A. "Hi" Busse and Eddie Martin
Used by Permission

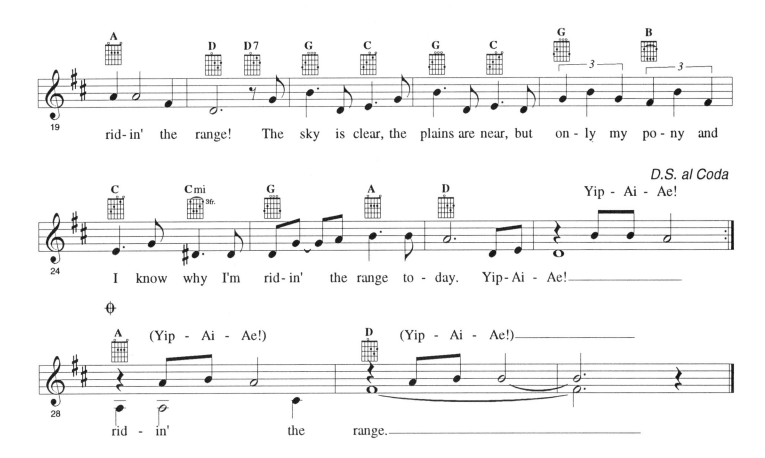

rid-in' the range! The sky is clear, the plains are near, but on-ly my po-ny and

I know why I'm rid-in' the range to-day. Yip-Ai-Ae!

D.S. al Coda

Yip-Ai-Ae!

(Yip-Ai-Ae!) (Yip-Ai-Ae!)

rid-in' the range.

Roy Rogers and the Mayor of New York, Mr. La Guardia c.1945 "Hi" and The Frontiersmen and part of Ray Whitley's band were the group. You can see just a part of Ray between Roy and the Mayor holding that Gibson guitar.

Rockin' and Rollin' in the Saddle

Words and Music by:
"Hi" Busse

© 1945 "Hi" Busse
Used by Permission

Hi there! brand there 'till the day is done;_____ ride, ride, ride_____ 'till the set - tin' of the sun;_____ ROCK - IN' AND ROLL - IN' IN THE SAD - DLE,_____ Sing - in' a song all day;_____ ROCK-IN' AND ROLL-IN' IN THE SAD-DLE,_____ Guess I was born that way._____

RIDIN' TO GLORY IN A NEW KIND OF GUN-FLAMING ROLE... AS RANGE SONGS RING!
Charles Starrett
THE MEDICO of PAINTED SPRINGS
TERRY WALKER and THE SIMP-PHONIES
A COLUMBIA PICTURE

Shooting up rustlers! Whooping up melodies! Rounding up a fresh brand of thrills...in a new kind of role!
CHARLES STARRETT
THE MEDICO OF PAINTED SPRINGS
TERRY WALKER ~ THE SIMP-PHONIES
A COLUMBIA PICTURE

Somewhere, Somehow

Words and Music by:
Eddie Martin and "Hi" Busse

With expression

(instrumental)

SOME - WHERE, SOME - WHERE, the suns' al - ways shin - ing down

on my home. SOME - HOW, SOME - HOW,

my heart is pin - ing for some - one to call my own.

Back in the hills of Wy - o - ming, Down in the

val - leys be - low, SOME - WHERE, SOME - HOW,

she will be wait - ing, Wait - in for me, I know.

© 1948 "Hi" Busse and Eddie Martin
Used by Permission

Daddy's Little Cowboy

Words and Music by:
Eddie Martin and "Hi" Busse

Tenderly

© 1948 "Hi" Busse and Eddie Martin
Used by Permission

Roll Wagons Roll

Written specifically as a theme for the Frontiersmen (still in use today)

Words and music by:
"Hi" Busse

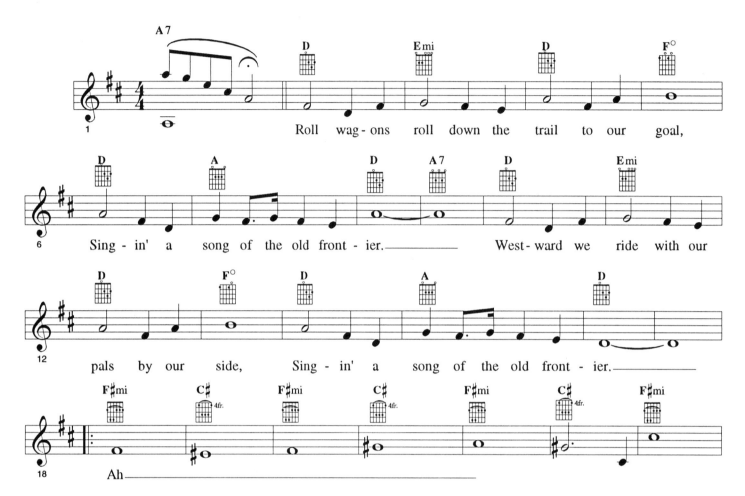

Roll wag-ons roll down the trail to our goal, Sing-in' a song of the old front-ier._____ West-ward we ride with our pals by our side, Sing-in' a song of the old front-ier._____

Ah_____

(Spoken) Well howdy, neighbors! I'm (HOST NAME)
speaking for the Frontiersmen, to sorta invite you t'ride
down the trail with us for the next fifteen minutes... with
songs of the old frontier! Join us, won't you?

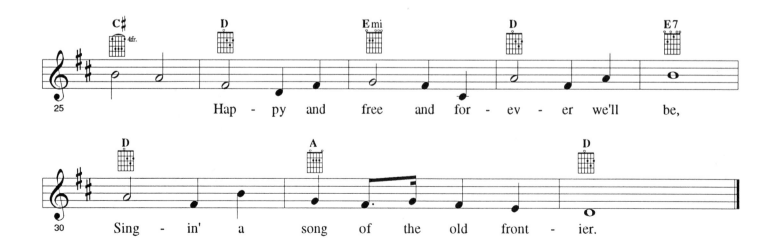

Hap-py and free and for-ev-er we'll be, Sing-in' a song of the old front-ier.

2.

know._____ I hear a voice a call in'

_____ call - in' me back to the range,_____

And now that the voice is call - in',

D.S. al Fine

I'm head - in' for a change, 'cause

The Frontiersmen, Hal Southern, Wayne West, Highpockets Busse c. 1955

Early 1970's, Left to right: Hal Southern (writer of Hillbilly Heaven), Pat Patterson, Rusty Richards, Hi Busse, and Ken "Festus" Curtis in front

"Hi" with Roy Rogers on tour 1945

Joey Bishop all dressed up in cowboy finery sings with The Frontiersmen backing him on the Joey Bishop show early 60's. Look at that <u>indoor</u> campfire!

Ray "Crash" Corrigan with two guns ablazing on the main street of Corriganville

Ray "Crash" Corrigan
CORRIGANVILLE

Corriganville Park (just north of Hollywood, California) was purchased by Ray "Crash" Corrigan in 1937 for $11,354. This actor/cowboy/stuntman fittingly named the property Corriganville and decided that the beautiful rocky landscape was the perfect setting for the filming of movies, especially westerns.

MOVIE RANCH
The development of the property as a private outdoor set could not have come at a better time as Hollywood was flooding the movie market with inexpensive "shoot-em-up" westerns. During this period, roads were developed, utilities were installed, wells were dug, trees were removed, a lake was formed, rock outcroppings were enhanced, and sets were constructed in and around the lowland areas to facilitate filming operations.

Throughout the 1940's and 1950's over 3000 movies were made using this dramatic scene. Corriganville also became the outdoor setting for many TV western series.

AMUSEMENT PARK
In 1949, Corrigan decided to convert the property into a commercial venture by developing a western amusement park that was open to the public. The park featured stuntmen shows, movie lots, a working western town, Indian crafts, stagecoach rides, pony rides and boating on a lake. During its heyday, the park attracted as many as 20,000 people on weekends and was rated among the top ten amusement parks in the United States.

SALE AND CLOSURE
Corriganville was purchased by Bob Hope in 1965 as part of a 1,400-acre land acquisition and was closed to the public a year later. A fire in 1970 caused extensive destruction to most of the movie sets and buildings.

RENEWED INTEREST
In 1988, 190 acres of land comprising the principal working areas of the original Corriganville Ranch were purchased by the City of Simi Valley, California for use as a Regional Park. This area soon became the focus of regional historical preservation efforts. The park has not yet opened.

Moon O'er Montana

Words and Music by:
Dan Meyer and Tom Spaulding

© 1991 Dan Meyer and Tom Spaulding
Used by Permission

20

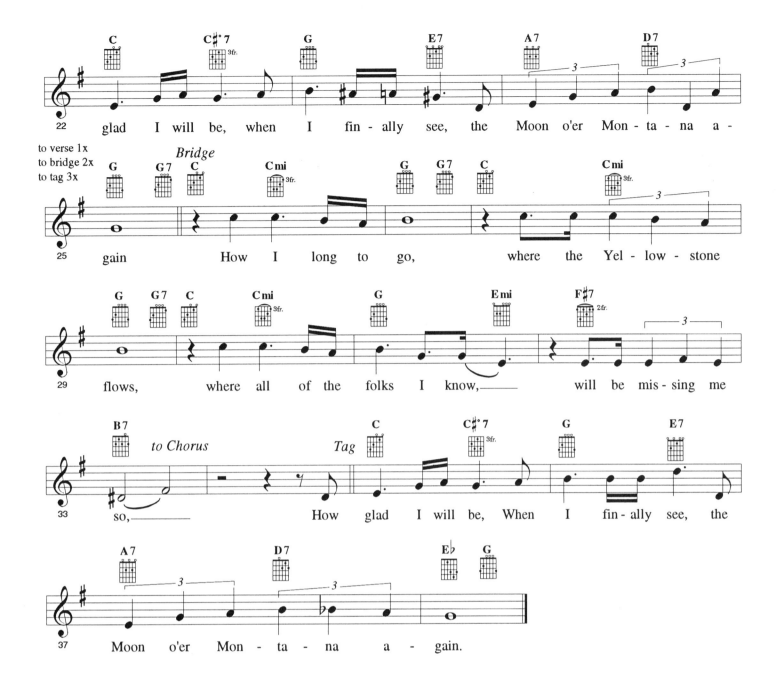

For more great music from
Montana Blue and the Big Sky Cowboys
send for their
CD or Cassette Tape
Carousel Records
P.O. Box 427
Sun Prairie, WI 53590

Ride 'em Cowboy

Words and Music by:
Dan Meyer and Robert Meyer

© 1991 Dan Meyer and Robert Meyer,
Used by Permission

spin - er, he's doomed with - out a clown._____ The

cow - boy and calls the bar - rel home._____ The

clown's bright cos - tume col - ors draw at - ten - tion from the

clown has lost the bat - tle but the bull has lost the

storm,_____ he's fen - cing with the bar - rel and his

war,_____ his pick - up men cor - ral him as the

clothes are loose and torn._____

M. C. tells the_____ score._____

Ragtime Cowboy Joe

Words by: Grant Clarke

Music by: Lewis F. Muir
and Maurice Abrahams

swings back and for - ward in the sad - dle On a horse that is syn - co - pat - ed, gait - ed. And there's such a fun - ny met - er to the roar of his re - peat - er, How they run when they hear the fel - low's gun, Be - cause the west - ern folks all know, He's a high fa - lu - ting, scoot - ing shoot - ing son - of - a - gun from Ar - i - zo - na, Rag - time, Cow - boy Joe. He al - ways Joe. -

Verse 2
Dressed up every Sunday in his Sunday clothes,
He beats it for the village where he always goes.
And every girl in town is Joe's.
'Cause he's a ragtime bear.
When he starts a Spieling on the dance hall floor,
No one but a lunatic would start a war.
Wise men know his forty-four
Makes men dance for fair.

Jingle, Jangle, Jingle

Moderato

Music by: Joseph J. Lilley
Words by: Frank Loesser

Copyright (c) 1942 (Renewed 1969) by Paramount Music Corporation
International Copyright Secured   All Rights Reserved

may have done some fool-in' This is why I nev-er fell, I got

spurs that jing-le jang - le jing-le_____ As I

go rid - in' mer-ri-ly a - long._____ And they

sing, "Oh ain't you glad you're sing - le!"_____ And that

song ain't so ver-y far from wrong._____ Oh, Mar - y

wrong so I'll jing - le on a - long._____

Yippeeay there'll be no weddin' bells, For today:

I got spurs that jingle, jangle, jingle
As I go ridin' merrily along.
And they sing, "Oh, ain't you glad you're single!"
And that song ain't so very far from wrong.

Oh, Lillie Belle Oh, Lillie Belle, Lillie Belle,
Though I many have done some foolin'
This is why I never fell,
I got spurs that jingle, jangle jingle
As I go ridin' merrily along.
And they sing, "Oh, ain't you glad you're single!"
And that song ain't so very far from wrong.

Oh Mary Ann, Oh, Mary Ann, Mary Ann,
Though we done some moon-light walkin
This is why I up and ran,
I got spurs that jingle, jangle jingle
As I go ridin' merrily along.
And they sing, "Oh, ain't you glad you're single!"
And that song ain't so very far from wrong.

Oh Sally Jane, Oh, Sally Jane, Sally Jane,
Though I'd love to stay forever,
This is why I can't remain,
I got spurs that jingle, jangle jingle
As I go ridin' merrily along.
And they sing, "Oh, ain't you glad you're single!"
And that song ain't so very far from wrong.

Oh, Bessie Lou, Oh, Bessie Lou, Bessie Lou,
Though we done a heap of dreamin'
This is why it won't come true,
I got spurs that jingle, jangle jingle
As I go ridin' merrily along.
And they sing, "Oh ain't you glad you're single!"
And that song ain't so very far from wrong.

27

End of the Line

Words and Music by:
Dan Meyer, Robert Meyer and Tom spaulding

© 1991 Dan Meyer, Robert Meyer and Tom Spaulding
Used by Permission

Montana Blue and the Big Sky Cowboys
top: Brian Meyer, Tom Spaulding, Dan Meyer
bottom: Bob Meyer, Kevin Meyer

Photo by David Loeb

High Country

Slowly

Words and Music by:
Bob Wagoner

© 1946 Bob Wagoner
Used by Permission

dreams _____ and a moun - tain of dreams _____

dreams _____ There I'll find a rain - bow,

_____ and a moun - tain of dreams _____

Robert Wagoner

I wrote " High Country" in 1946. I was in the Marine Corps, 18 years old and a military policeman stationed at the maximum security naval prison on Terminal Island in Southern California. While on my guard post walking a catwalk late one night, I was looking through the barbed wire listening to the ocean and wishing I was up in the High Sierra where I had spent much of my youth fishing and hiking the back country. The words of the song are the thoughts that were in my mind that night. I just wrote them down and put them to music.

When I was discharged from the Marines I headed back to the "High Country" and vowed to someday live there. Although I had to spend many years in the city working in construction, I finally made it back to the mountains for good in 1971 where I now have my art and music studio. It was the best move I ever made.

Hear the multi-talented
Robert Wagoner
on these cassettes tapes
"Heart Of The Golden West"
"Chant Of The Wanderer"
To order:
High Country Recording
P.O. Box 213
Bishop, CA 93514

Singing cowboy Ray Whitley
with his coustom built
Gibson J-200 guitar

33

Timberline

Words and Music by
Tom Chambers

©1989 How The West Was Sung, Music Publishing
Used by Permission

Her breath forms the mist in the morn - in'. She's laugh - in' when camp rob - bers sing. Tim - ber - line my Tim - ber - line in the land of the col - um - bine I'll soon re - turn home nev - er more roam from the la - dy I call Tim - ber - line.

Tom Chambers

Verse 2
In the summer she flaunts all her beauty to the warmth of the southwestern sun.
In autumn she dons her aspens of gold to warn of the season to come.
For winter she's wrapped up in ermine with moonbeams she'll sparkle and glow.
Halo of clouds, a necklace of pine she's embraced by the soft silent snow.
If ever again I can join her, I'll beed no more to stray from that pine-covered gal in the Rockies who stole my heart away.

CHORUS,
TAG

Buck Page

Buck Page and his original Riders Of The Purple Sage have been cutting a trail of music since 1936. Buck says he formed the group that year to play coast to coast for NBC's KDKA Radio. The original lineup consisted of Bob Parker on guitar, Ken Cooper on accordion, Hal McCoy on string bass and Buck on guitar, banjo, and fiddle. Buck says *"My brother Hilary was a Zane Grey addict and when he got married he left most of the books he had read by Zane Grey at home with me. I was looking for a name for my new group and came across the book Riders of the Purple Sage and I thought what a great name for my new band"*.

Their unique blends of harmony, and true western songs, have made them part of our musical heritage. The Riders, along with Gene Autry, Roy Rogers, Tex Ritter, Rex Allen, The Son's Of The Pioneers, and others, brought Western music to the nation by way of radio, stage, the silver screen, and finally television.

The Riders were one of the first to make big hits out of "Ghost Riders In The Sky", "Don't Fence Me In", "Blue Shadows On The Trail", and "Along The Santa Fe Trail", and many others.

Buck started in radio at the age of 11 and has been a rancher most of his life, raising, riding and racing horses: all the while playing and writing some great western songs about the cowboy life. As an actor he has appeared in over 200 motion pictures including, "The Glenn Miller Story", and "A Star Is Born" with Judy Garland. As a studio musician Buck played lead guitar on the theme songs for "Bonanza" "Laramie", "Wagon Train", and "77 Sunset Strip". He has served on staff at all three major networks and studied music at the Los Angeles Conservatory of Music.

Riders of the Purple Sage, Buck Page on right c. 1940

Rollin' Rollin' Prairies

Words and Music by:
Buck Page

© 1990 Buck Page
Used by Permission

Moonlight on the Canyon

Words and Music by:
Buck Page

© 1994 Buck Page
Used by Permission

Out 'Neath the Western Sky

Words and Music by:
Buck Page

© 1994 Buck Page
Used by Permission

Back to the Hills of Wyoming

Words and Music by:
Buck Page

© 1994 Buck Page
Used by Permission

say - ing,_____ get up son and hoe the corn._____

When I get back to Wy - om - ing,_____ I'll ne - ver more roam this world._____

_____ So it's back to the hills of Wy - om - ing,_____ And you

sweet lit - tle girl._____

D.C. al fine

"Red River" Dave with the Riders at The Village Barn, New York City, Feburary 1940. left: Buck is playing the fiddle, Ken Cooper, Bob Parker, and Hal McCoy

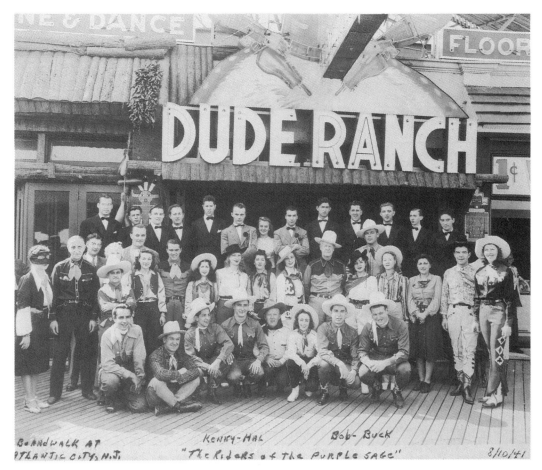

The Dude Ranch, Atlantic City, New Jersey, August 1941

Buck Page and
"The Original Riders of the Purple Sage"

Buck Page, Ron Jones,
and Joe (J.B.) Boemecke

42

TEX RITTER

Woodward Maurice Ritter, was born in Murvaul, Texas on January 12, 1905, the youngest of 6 children. He spent the years in Murvaul, then moved to Nederland and Beaumont Texas were he attended school. He studied law at the University of Texas at Austin in 1922. While in college, he debated on the Oratory Society, acted in plays, sang in the Choral Society and Glee Club. For a time he had his own program singing cowboy songs on a Houston radio station. Tex became lifelong friends with J. Frank Dobie, the writer and historian of Southwestern folk-lore, and Oscar J. Fox, director of the Glee Club and composer of Western songs; through these contacts, Tex became the only one of the singing cowboys who actually was schooled in the music of the West. The title of his show was The Texas Cowboy and His Songs.

Over the next five years, in New York, Tex had a job in a men's chorus of the Broadway operetta, *The New Moon*. In 1930, he was casted as Cord Elam, one of the singing cow-boys in the play, *Green Grow The Lilacs*. Today *Green Grow The Lilacs* is best remem-bered as the play upon which Rodgers and Hammerstein's classic Broadway musical, *Oklahoma* was based. He also had a part in another Broadway play, *The Round Up*. He appeared on radio programs including *The Lone Star Rangers, Cowboy Tom's Round-up* and the *WHN Barn Dance*. He also recorded five songs for the American Record Corporation (which later became Columbia Records) all between October 1932 and March 1933.

In 1936 Tex went to Hollywood to star in a movie *Song of the Gringo*. The film was a success and Tex went on to make 11 more for Grand National, including *Arizona Days, Sing Cowboy Sing, and Trouble in Texas,* with leading lady Rita Cansino (later changed name to Rita Hayworth). In 1938 Tex signed with Monogram and over the next three years starred in 20 films including, *Where the Buffalo Roam* and *Sundown on the Prairie,* and *Song of the Buckaroo,* which featured an actress named Dorothy Fay, they were mar-ried in June 1941.

Tex recorded for Decca Records between 1935 and 1939, with little success. In 1942 he recorded for Capitol, were he remained for life. His first recording on June 11, 1942 was "Jingle, Jangle, Jingle". Hits such as "There's a New Moon Over my Shoulder, " "Jealous Heart," "You Will Have to Pay," and "Rye Whiskey," along with albums of cow-boy songs and recitations, "Deck of Cards" and "The Pledge of Allegiance." During these years, Tex and Dorothy's sons, Tom and John, were born. They lived on a ranch in Van Nuys, in Los Angeles' San Fernando Valley.

In 1952 the film "High Noon" became one of the year's biggest hits, starring Gary Cooper and Grace Kelly. The film went on to win Academy Awards for best musical score and best song and Tex performed the song on that year's Oscar telecast. On May 14, 1952, Tex Ritter went into the studio with the ballad that became his trademark.

Tex recorded for Decca Records between 1935 and 1939, with little success. In 1942 he recorded for Capitol, were he remained for life. His first recording on June 11, 1942 was "Jingle, Jangle, Jingle". Hits such as "There's a New Moon Over my Shoulder, " "Jealous Heart," "You Will Have to Pay," and "Rye Whiskey," along with albums of cowboy songs and recitations, "Deck of Cards" and "The Pledge of Allegiance." During these years, Tex and Dorothy's sons, Tom and John, were born. They lived on a ranch in Van Nuys, in Los Angeles' San Fernando Valley.

In 1952 the film "High Noon" became one of the year's biggest hits, starring Gary Cooper and Grace Kelly. The film went on to win Academy Awards for best musical score and best song and Tex performed the song on that year's Oscar telecast. On May 14, 1952, Tex Ritter went into the studio with the ballad that became his trademark.

When the Country Music Association was formed in 1958, Tex became one of its charter members. In 1963 he became its president and played an important role in developing the organization and raising money to house The Hall Of Fame Museum. In 1964 he was elected to the Hall of Fame, the first Western performer to be so honored.

In 1965 he moved to Nashville to co-host with Ralph Emery on WSM's late-night radio show. He was also a regular performer on the Opry.

On January 2, 1974 he was struck down by a heart attack, ten days before his 69th birthday.

TEX RITTER TRAIL NEWS

Vol. IV   SUMMER ISSUE   1948

"Tex Ritter and White Flash"

"The Tex Ritter Trail News,"
for members of the Tex Ritter Fan clubs

Blood On the Saddle

Made popular by Tex Ritter, this song was written in Arizona in the 1920s by Everett Cheatam and Romaine Lowdermilk. A particularly bad rodeo accident is said to have inspired this gory song.

There was blood on the sad - dle._____ There was blood

all a - round,_____ And a great big pud - dle_____

_____ of blood on the ground._____

A cowboy lay in it,
All covered with gore.
And he never will ride
Any broncos no more.

O pity the cowboy
All bloody and red.
For a bronco fell on him,
And mashed in his head.

There was blood on the saddle.
There was blood all around.
And a great big puddle
Of blood on the ground.

EDWARD L ALPERSON
PRESENTS

TEX RITTER
IN
ROLLIN' PLAINS

AN EDWARD FINNEY
PRODUCTION
A GRAND NATIONAL PICTURE

Arizona Home

(Linda's Song)

Words and Music by:
John Ryberg

I've crossed the prai-ries and I've flown to-ward the sun; I've wan-dered far to where the deep wa-ters run. I've seen the Nor-thern Lights, I've heard the sea-birds' song, But Ar-i-zo-na's still where I be-long. I want to see the world, to look a-round the bend; My bags are al-ways packed, my heart is in the wind. But not long af-ter I have touched a dis-tant land I know that I'm a child of the de - sert sand.

Deep rocky canyon, where the summer waters flow;
High mountain ridges, white with first winter snow
Sloping Bajada, covered withe the cactus thorn;
The Sonoran Desert is, the place where I was born.

Es Maravilloso when you see the monsoon come;
Es Infierno when you feel the desert sun;
Unico sitio saguaros touch the sky;
La Hedionidilla aroma almost makes me cry.

Ajo, Nogales, Arivada, Patagon'
Sonoita Tubao, Tumacacori y Tucson
Yo Amo Baja Arizona, Mi Hogar
en Baja Arizona, Quiero Cantar.

© 1988 John A. Ryberg II
Used by Permission

Ride in the Wind

Words and Music by:
John Ryberg

I'm rid-in' hard a-long the Mo-gol-lon,____ Push-in' my po-ny cuz I'm head-in' home.____ It's been a long ride but my spir-its' bright,____ I'm go-in' danc-in' with my gal to-night.____ Ride, Ride, Ride, Ride in the wind, Let my ol' po-ny have his head let 'im ro-am.

Ride,_____ Ride in the wind, I'm rid-in' hard I'm head-in home.

Verse 2
This roundup lasted more the thirty days;
A thousand branded with a couple hundred strays;
Rope 'em, burn 'em, cut 'em, set 'em, free;
It's time to head bck to the Circle T.

(Chorus)

Verse 3
The sun is setting in a fiery haze;
She's down there waitin' with an anxious gaze;
I hear the fiddles playin' 'neath the canyon rim;
I'll swing my lady as the light grows dim.

(Chorus)

Verse 4
By the next roundup, when I have to ride;
That little Gal is gonna be my bride;
I know that she'll be waitin' on the canyon rim;
And I'll be Ridin' in the Wind.

THE DESERT SONS

Benny Young, Darrel Yarbrough, John Ryberg

© 1992 John A. Ryberg II
Used by Permission

47

CODE OF THE WEST

We were singing at the Gene Autry Museum and I saw a code there he tried to live by.. I took his points and added some and put them to music. You know this is the code we tried to live by then and still makes sense today

Words and Music by:
John C. Lamont

This is the code of the west. My Saturday heros put life to the test. The way to judge wrong and tell right from the rest, by living the code of the west.

(Codes)
One / Two / Three / Four
Five / Six / Seven / Eight
Nine / Seven / Eleven / Twelve

1. Never take (unfair) advantage
2. Be trustworthy and loyal too
3. Be kind to animals and nature's creatures
4. Have no racial or religious prejudices

Chorus: (Gene, Roy and Hoppy)

6. Be industrious and work for good
7. Be helpful to elders and others in need
8. Be respectful to all womanhood

Chorus: (Dale, Gail and Annie)

9. Be patriotic and fight for justice
10. Give time to others and do your part
11. Always have cleanliness of thought and speech
12. Do your best with a grateful heart

Last chorus:
This is my code of the west
The way that I choose to put life to the test
The way I judge wrong and tell right from the rest
I'm living the code of the west

© 1993 John C. Lamont
Used by Permission

48

alamo

(Sp *alamo*: cottonwood tree, poplar; Texas and SW). *Populus monilifera.*
This simple Spanish word for poplar is surely the most evocative in the American language, for it gave its name to the old Spanish mission fort built in 1756 within sight of San Antonio de Bexar.

alforja

(Mex-Sp). A saddlebag, a bag, a bag to hang on either side of a pack-saddle. Anglicized as **alforche, alforge, alforka, alforki,** with *alforje* as a respectable Mexican variant.

apple

A saddlehorn. A real disgrace to **grab the apple** or **pull leather** when trying to stay on a wild one.

Arbuckle

(1) A generic term for coffee, taken by cattlemen from the trade-name paramount throughout the West. (Ramon Adams 1944; Foster-Harris 1955) Also **Arbuckle's.**
(2) A greenhorn cowhand said to have been obtained by the boss in exchange for premium stamps given away with cans of coffee.

Arizona   nightingale

A burro, a donkey.

armas

(Mex-Sp) A forerunner of chaps which were little more than two large flaps of hide fastened to the saddle and protecting a rider's legs against brush and thorns.   Not to be confused with armitas, which were worn by the rider, not the horse.

arroyo

(Mex-Sp; SW). Also **arroya** (Wentworth 1944). A deep-sided watercourse, usually cut in a soft surface, with or without water in it. In Arizona, for much of the year they were dry, when they were referred to as **arroyos secos.**

balling up

Referred to bunching up by cattle--at a river-crossing or entrance to a corral, for example. It was usual for a large herd to be broken up into smaller bunches to prevent this from happening.

bandana

(from the Hindi *bandhnyu,* via Eastern United States). Also **bandanna.** The neckerchief of the cowman. Folded in a triangle to tie at the front or back, according to taste. Often of cotton but preferably of silk, which was cool in summer and warm in winter; bright colors and spots were favored. It served endless uses: it covered the neck above an often collarless shirt, masked mouth and nostrils against dust, filtered foul water, and tied down hat brims over the ears during cold weather. If you wanted to rob a bank or hold up a stage without being recognized, it could serve as a mask. Those who know have questioned whether the word was much used by cow-country men.

bar-bit

A straight or nearly straight bit for a horse's mouth, at either end of which is a ring for the bridle and reins.

barbwire

Two inventions brought about the end of different eras in the West. One was the repeating firearm, the effect of which was dramatic enough; the other was barbwire, the effect of which was not only dramatic but traumatic. It was simply fence wire with barbs on it, the commonest designs consisting of two wires twisted together with the barbs themselves twisted a number of times and in various ways around the wire. Within a decade of its introduction in the 1860's it changed the character of the wide-open ranges of the West. Its effect upon the economics and upon the social and workaday habits and customs of the Western folk was abrupt and final: with it, the old days went. What the term *Old West* fully stood for was gone.

    The story and facts of this wicked-looking wire are impressive and astonishing; the variety of types and the tonnage produced to meet the insatiable demand are staggering. Osgood 1929, for example, quotes impressive production figures starting at five tons in 1874, and mounting steadily year by year to 200,000 tons annually in 1900, the last year of our period. In 1884 Charles Goodnight and friends ran a fence from Indian Territory across the Panhandle and thirty-five miles into New Mexico. The numbers of patents issued on an extraordinary variety of designs are equally astonishing; starting modestly with 11 patents in the years 1868-73, the figures climb steadily to 94 in the years 1881-85, and make a total of 306 patents in 17 years.

    All you could want to know on this subject is to be found in Glover 1972. (Mr. Glover publishes his authoritative material from what I consider to be the most colorfully named press in the world - The Cow Puddle Press of Sunset, Texas.) He writes: "The beginning of the need for barbed wire was seen in the year 1867 as a few men applied, that year, for patents pertaining to restraining wire with sharp points to turn and hold livestock." Most of the early manufacturers were established in Iowa, Illinois, and areas near enough to the Great Plains to be aware of stock and range problems that had not been solved by the smooth wire produced as early as 1853 (the Meriwether type, patented at New Braunfels, Texas). A good many men patented designs of "thorny fence" before the famous Joseph Glidden, who, with good organization, plant, and franchises, rose to be the chief manufacturer by 1885.

    Barbwire was the answer to all those who wished to keep their range from outsiders on the treeless plains where there was little timber for fencing. Ranchers used it to stop cattle from drifting (and lived to regret it bitterly when the animals died by the thousands when prevented from escaping the worst effects of winter during the great die-ups; they planted wire to stop other men from using precious water sources; some strung wire to block trails; farmers fenced crops in and cattle out. In fact, whole towns were cut off by cattlemen hastily encircling ranges.

    Many powerful ranchers were passionate open-rangers, but when the mighty **XIT** outfit of the Texas Panhandle went in for the stuff in a big way, most of them were convinced that the old days had gone. Shorthorn cows were coming in and they could not walk twenty miles to water as could the old Longhorns. Also they were more valuable. Barbwire had become an economic necessity, and the cowboy was downgraded from the historic herdsman on horseback to a laborer whose spade, pick, hammer, and pliers were now as important as his rope, gun and branding iron.

barefooted

Said of a horse that was unshod. Indians rode such horses, though they also shod horses with rawhide. The mustangs of the hills developed hard feet and could run on rock and hard ground without injury to them

bat wing chaps

Also **bat wings** (Ramon Adams 1944), **Texas wing chaps,** *winged chaps.* Chaps with wide wings, so wide that they were easy to put on and pull off when the wearer was booted and spurred.

bedding down

The act of cattle-drovers bringing the herd to rest, a process that had to be carried out with skill and precision if the semi-wild Longhorns were to pass a peaceful night.

bed-ground

Also **bedding-ground.** Area selected for bedding-down cattle at night on a trail-drive. This might be chosen by the trail-boss or by the cook, who usually went ahead of the slow-moving herd to find a good campsite and to prepare the evening meal.

-continued on page 60-

Old Spanish Trail

The old Spanish trail extended from Los Angeles up through Las Vegas Nevada, St. George, Utah then farther North then East into New Mexico. Upon contemplating our move to St. George and leaving California I wondered what Spanish influence that area might have had. I've spent so much time writing and reading about California vaqueros and history that I wanted to create a song about our new home to be.

Words and Music by:
John C. Lamont

Have you ev-er been to U-tah? On the old——Spain-ish trail.

Seen the Rock-ies kiss the heav-ens heard the love Lo-bo wail?——

— Have you ev-er been to U-tah? You ought to know (You ought to

go) That the vir-gin riv-er val-ley makes me want to take a dal-ly on a fil-ly there I know.

That the vir-gin riv-er val-ley make me want to take a dal-ly on a fil-ly there I know.

ending (last time) *inst.*

(know)——

© 1992 John C. Lamont
Used by Permission

Have you ever been to Utah
On the old Spanish Trail,
Seen the rockies kiss the heavens,
Heard the lone lobo wail?

Have you ever been to Utah?
You ought to know (you ought to know)
That the virgin river valley
makes me want to take a dally
On a filly there I know.
That the virgin river valley
Make me want to take a dally
On a filly there I know.

Even Los conquistadors
Searching for cities of gold,
Couldn't help but see the beauty
In painted brush strokes so bold.

That's not why I go to Utah
You ought to know
That the blue in the skies
Is the blue in her eyes
That is why I must go.
"Cause the blue in the skies
Is the blue in her eyes
That is why I must go.

John and Sharron Lamont

Rydin' High Cassette Tapes:
"Out California Way"
"Song of the Californio"
to order:
Rydin' High
3606 Hatch Road - Merced, CA 95340

51

Old California

I tried to put into words and music for my lovely state and it's wonderful history. The cowboy was not invented in Texas as some of you may believe. The came from the California Vaquero!

Words and Music by:
John C. Lamont

Old Cal - i - forn - ia   your   name e - vokes vis - ions of

old Span - ish miss - ions of Pat - i - os and moon - light fi - es - tas

Old   Cal - i - forn - ia   bright -

eyed sen - or - i - tas Ay si mi chi - qui - tas   mus - ic and mid - day si -

est - as   You   are   the   heart   and   the

soul   of   my   song: El   Al   ma   de   mi   can - cion.

Since   I   first   met   you

© 1992 John C. Lamont
Used by Permission

I can't for-get you mi a-mor y mi cora-zon

thoughts they grow fond-er Cal-i-forn-ia you are my home.

Old California
Your name evokes visions of old Spanish missions
Of patios and moonlight fiestas.
Old California
Bright-eyed señoritas, ay sí mis chiquitas,
Music and midday siestas.

Chorus:
You are the heart and the soul of my song
El alma de Mi canción.
Since I first met you, I can't forget you
Mi amor Y mi corazón.

Old California
Your bold vaqueros and prod caballeros,
Horsemen of daring and mystery.
Old California
Land of plenty, of gold, of glorious history.

Chorus:
You are the heat and the soul of my song
El alma de mi canción.
I see in your face both beauty and grace
Mi amor Y mi canción.

Old California
You work your cattle with center-fire saddle
Reata and long tapadero.
Old California
No one compares to the skill of your old-time vaquero.

Chorus:
You are the heart and the soul of my song
El alma de mi canción.
Your vision is calling as night it is falling
Mi amor Y mi canción.

Though I may wander,
Your memory grows fonder
California--you are my home
California--you are my home.

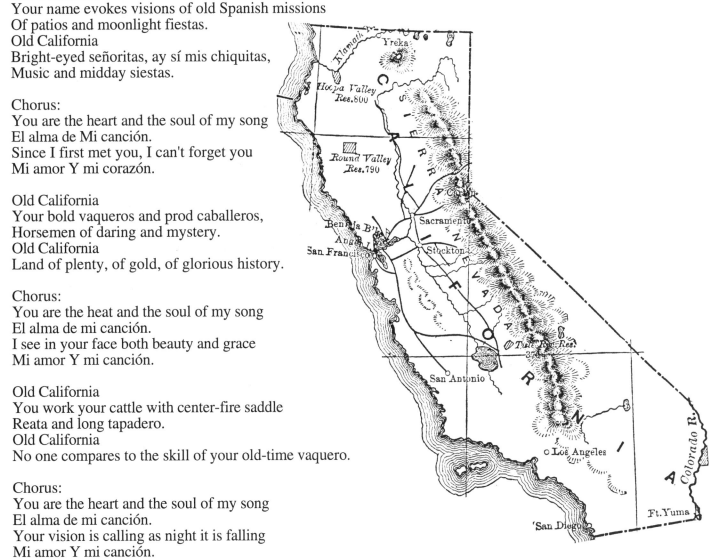

**California reproduced here
was published by Harper's in August 1874.**

CARSON ROBISON
profile by Dave Bourne

I like Carson Robison because he wrote "Little Green Valley". That song alone gets him into my personal hall of fame. To me that tune has always stood pre-eminate in what I like to call bucolic/nostalgia, serenades. "Carry Me Back To The Lone Prairie", another Robison tune is a pretty fair example of a good cowboy song. His most famous songs, "Barnacle Bill The Sailor", and "Life Gets Tee-jus" indicate just what a wide range of styles of which he was capable.

Born Carson (after the scout Kit Carson), Jay Robison in Oswego, Kansas on August 4, 1890, he grew up in Chetopa,15 miles south of Oswego. His father played the fiddle and called square dances. Carson played guitar, tenor banjo, ukulele, and sang. He was also a champion whistler and could warble in 3rds with the best of 'em. He was really an excellent rhythm guitar player, as his subsequent studio tenure will testify.

He worked on farms, ranches, and in the oil fields prior to 1920, when at the age of 30 "he decided that he would rather starve in the music business than get rich in the oil business". He went to the nearest large city, Kansas City, and worked on radio as a popular musician. While in Kansas City, he played theaters with the Kansas City Nighthawks, and the Coon-Saunders Band.

In 1924 he went to New York to whistle on a couple of Wendell Hall records and remained based there for the rest of his life. He worked for Victor Records as a studio guitarist for many years, working with such people as Gene Austin, ("My Blue Heaven"), comediane Frank Crumit, and also with the Roy Smeck Trio. He was well know for writing "disaster" and "event" tunes like "Wreck of the Number Nine", many of which were recorded by Vernon Dahlhart. He is credited with writing about 300 songs.

During the 20's, he sort of pioneered duet singing first when he was brought in to aid Vernon Dahlhart's lagging career and later with Frank Luther. In the 30's Robison made his first commitment to the western image with the formation of Carson Robison's Buckaroos. Along with Frank Novak, Pearl, John, and Bill Mitchell, they performed on radio and traveled the English speaking world from Europe to New Zealand. He had begun to lose his hair at an early age, and with Mitchell family being a generation younger, he was rarely seen without a cowboy hat from the 30's on. At heart, Carson always fancied himself a cowboy and was rarely photographed in later years without western dress. In his last years he called himself the "Kansas City Jayhawk". His horse "Prince", a gelding which was just over 16 hands high, was his pride and joy. He also kept cattle and chickens. At least one son was a multi-talented instrumentalist, reportedly playing 22 instruments. Carson died on March 24, 1957 in Poughkeepsie, New York.

Robison has been largely over looked by contemporary musicologists largely because his career was so varied. It's hard to pigeon hole his music because he wrote and played in so many different styles. Country, cowboy, western, old timey, pop, mountain, folk, mmm hard to say . . probably all of these. One writer characterized him as the first of the "rural professionals". It was nice to hear a country (as in "out in the country") type musician who performed rural music without a twang in his accent, without a nasal tone, and who could actually tune and play his instrument. In an interview several years ago, Wilf Carter expressed the view that Carson Robison was more deserving of the title of "Father of Country Music" than Jimmie Rodgers. At the very least, he certainly played an important role in bringing a type of music to the radio, and world stage that had been previously ignored.

Photo Courtesy of Ray Avery

Carson Robison (holding bass) & The Buckaroos

Gently Does the Trick

Carson J. Robinson

Come all and hear me sing, A song both good and wise, I'll

make the can-yon ring, With val-u-'ble ad-vice, In go-ing thro' this

world, You'll find it rare-ly wrong, To keep a stead-y pace, And

keep on go-ing strong. Chorus: For it's gent-ly, soft-ly,

slow-ly does the trick,—— Get on eas-y, care-ful, nev-er be too

quick, The breeze fresh from the pas-ture may not be a speed-y last-er, So it's

gent-ly does the trick.————

1. Come all and hear me sing, A song both good and wise,
I'll make the canyon ring, With valu'ble advice,
In going thro' this world, You'll find it rarely wrong,
To keep a steady pace, And keep on going strong.

Chorus:
For it's gently, softly, slowly does the trick,
Get on easy, careful, never be too quick,
The breeze fresh from the pasture may not be a speedy laster,
So it's gently does the trick.

2. Now if in prison you, should happen for to land,
For picking up a steer, That bears a strangers brand,
Be gentle, meek and mild, In that way you may gain,
But if you act up rough, You'll wear the ball and chain.

Chorus:

3. For it's gently, softly, slowly does the trick,
You'll walk clanky, hobbledy, not so very quick,
They keep your legs in order and you'd softly cuss the warder,
Saying gently does the trick.

4. Or if a bronco bucks, And lifts you in the air,
You have a kind of feel, You'd rather not be there,
Your eleration feels. Well, anything but nice,
But don't you be afraid, Just take a friends advice.

Chorus:
Came down gently, softly, slowly does the trick,
Just fall easy, careful, never be too quick,
Your eye the distance gauges, so you land by easy stages,
For it's gently does the trick.

M.M. COLE EDITION

of

Carson J. Robison's

World's Greatest Collection of

Mountain Ballads *and* Old Time Songs

with Words and Music — Guitar Chords Piano Accompaniment

CONTAINS 50 Big Hits

such as

Hallelujah I'm a Bum
Dying Cowboy
Golden Slippers
Birmingham Jail
When the Work's All Done This Fall
She'll Be Comin' 'Round the Mountain
East Bound Train
Bury Me Out on the Prairie
Letter Edged in Black
Hand Me Down My Walking Cane
Also Guitar Chords.

PRICE 75¢

Published by M.M. Cole Publishing House ~~~~~ Chicago

The Hell Bound Train

A Texas cowboy's drunken nightmare of the devil and a soul to sell, and how he prayed to be saved from a train ride to hell

Carson J. Robinson

A Tex-as cow-boy on a bar-room floor had drank so much he could hold no more, so he fell a-sleep with a trou-bled brain, to dream that he rode on the Hell-bound train, The en-gine with mur-der-ous blood was damp, the head-light was a big brim-stone lamp, While an Imp, for fuel,——was shov-'ling bones, The fur-nance rang with a thous-and groans.

I only got one bullet left, . . . so line up single file, facin' ME!

58

The boiler was filled full of lager beer,
And the devil himself was the engineer,
The passengers were a mixed up crew,
Church member, Atheist, Gentile and Jew,
The rich man in broad cloth, the poor in rags,
Handsome girls and wrinkled hags,
While black men, yellow men, red and white.
All chained together a fearful sight.

The train rushed on at an awful pace
The sulphurous fumes scorched their hands and face,
Wilder and wilder the country grew,
And faster and faster the engine flew,
Louder and louder the thunder crashed,
And brighter and brighter the lightning flashed,
Hotter and hotter the air became,
Til the clothes were burnt from each shrinking frame.

Then out of the distance there rose a yell,
"Ha ha," said the devil, "the next stop's hell."
Then oh, how the passengers shrieked with pain,
And begged the devil to stop the train,
But he capered about and danced with glee,
And laughed and mocked at their misery,
"My friends you paid for your seats on this road,
The train goes through with the complete load."

You've bullied the weak and cheated the poor,
The starving brother turned from your door,
You've laid up gold tell your purses bust,
And given free play to your beastly lust.
You've paid full fare and I'll carry you through,
For it's only right and should have your due,
The laborer always expects his hire,
So I'll land you safe in the lake of fire.

Your flesh will scorch in the flames that roar,
And my imps torment you for evermore,
Then the cowboy woke was an anguished cry,
His clothes were wet and his hair stood high,
Then he prayed as he never prayed before,
To be saved from his sins and hell's front door,
His prayers and pleadings were not in vain,
For he never rode on the hell bound train.

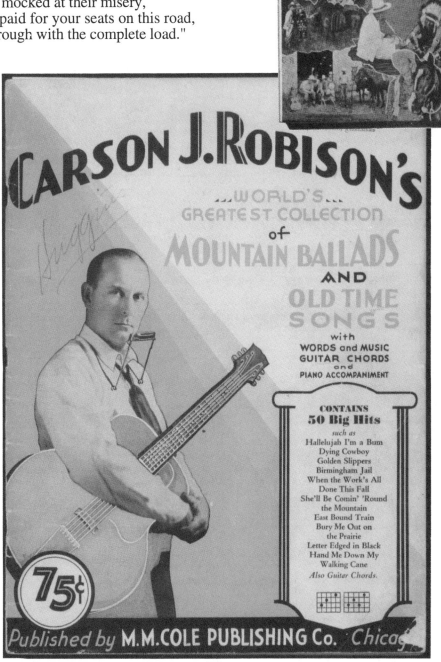

CARSON ROBISON'S "CR" Ranch Song Folio

Under the personal supervision of CARSON ROBISON

CARSON J. ROBISON'S
...WORLD'S...
GREATEST COLLECTION
of
MOUNTAIN BALLADS
AND
OLD TIME SONGS

with
WORDS and MUSIC
GUITAR CHORDS
and
PIANO ACCOMPANIMENT

CONTAINS
50 Big Hits
such as
Hallelujah I'm a Bum
Dying Cowboy
Golden Slippers
Birmingham Jail
When the Work's All
Done This Fall
She'll Be Comin' 'Round
the Mountain
East Bound Train
Bury Me Out on
the Prairie
Letter Edged in Black
Hand Me Down My
Walking Cane
Also Guitar Chords.

75¢

Published by M.M.COLE PUBLISHING Co. Chicago

THE "COW CHIP" JINGLE

Though all of us might try our best,
We can't bring back the Wild West.
But there's one thing that can remind us,
Of those treasured days behind us,
Of stories told around the fire,
Of horses that would never tire,
While cattle grazed the meadows green,
With fences few and far between.
That's where the cow chip came about,
The cookie that made cowboys shout.
From miles around you'd hear them hoot,
"Ya whoo! What's that on my boot?!!"
They quickly spread throughout the land,
In answer to the high demand.
And to this day they haven't changed,
They still come fresh from the open range!
©1982 Butter Creek Farms

Cowboy Tidbits

bed-roll

Also **bedding roll.** A cowhand's bed, usually consisting of a tarp(tarpaulin) and blankets. In the later days, the tarp was sometimes called a **paulin.** Later too the bed-roll might contain a sougan , a quilted cover. This roll contained most of the cowboy's possessions.

bed-wagon

Also *hoodlum,* **hoodlum wagon.** A wagon that carried the bed-rolls and other equipment on the trail. A later development and only used by the larger outfits on long drives. Generally such tackle was carried on the chuck wagon.

bible

A cowhand's cigarette papers.

Bible-puncher

Usually a preacher, ordained or not, but also a religious man who quoted the holy text.

Bible Two

The second Bible of the Texas Rangers, which provided them each year with a list of wanted men and was therefore read by them more avidly than Bible One.

big antelope

A man might so refer to a cow when he had killed it for food knowing that it belonged to another man. There was a saying that only a fool ate his own beef.

big jaw

A cattle disease found among the Longhorns

big loop

Also **wide loop.** The loop of a cow-thief's lasso, said to be so big that, when thrown, it landed on other men's cattle.

biscuit

The saddlehorn.

biscuit-roller

A cook.

blab

Also **blab board.** A board attached to a calf's nose to prevent it from suckling while being weaned.

black cattle

The cattle of early Texas, not to be confused with the Longhorns, but nevertheless possessing long horns which they well knew how to use. In the brush-country, they were referred to as *cimarrones* (wild ones), as were the Longhorns. They were usually black (these were also known as *mustang cattle*), but not always, for they could be marked by a light dorsal stripe. Such line-backed cattle, according to Dobie 1941, were also called *zorrillas* (polecats).

-continued on page 68-

60

A Prisoner For Life

His crime is never disclosed, but his sorrow is easy to understand: his absence from a loved one-
"nevermore shall my eyes by your beauty be blessed"- his envy of the birds-"just to roam at my
ease, just to breathe the fresh air."

Verse 2
Farewell, little birdies
That fly in the sky,
You fly all day long
And sing your troubles by;
What would I give
Such freedom to share,
To roam at ease
And breathe the fresh air;

Verse 3
I would roam through the cities,
Through village and dell,
But I never would return
To my cold prison cell.
I'm the downfall of my family,
My children, my wife;
God pity and pardon
The poor prisoner for life.

An Old Dusty Saddle

Words and Music by:
J.L. Frank, Pee Wee King
and Milton Estes

His face was worn and wrink-led, His hair had turned to gray, He was an old time cow-hand, That lived in yes-ter-day, He said he had a treas-ure He'd keep un-til he died, And when I asked him what it was This old cow-hand re-plied.

Chorus There's an old dus-ty sad-dle That hangs on the wall, It's cov-ered with

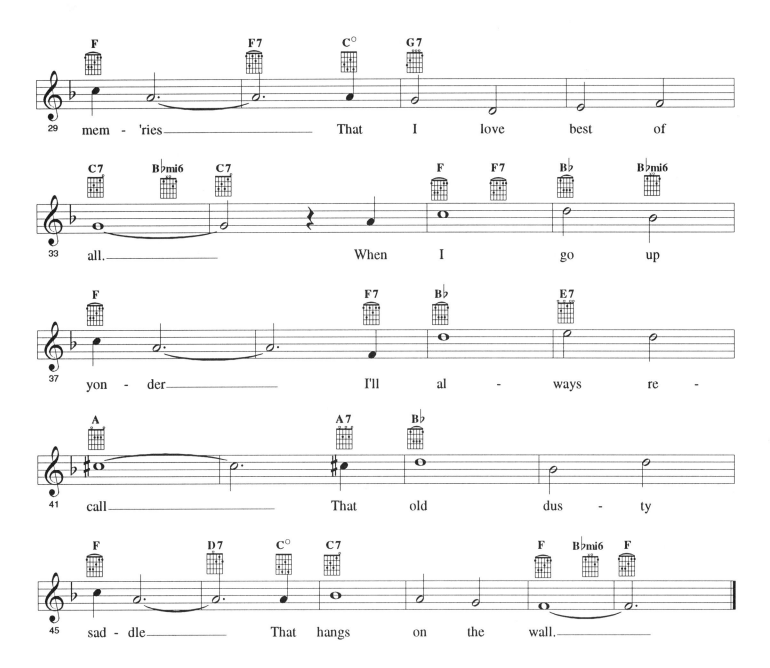

29 mem - 'ries_____ That I love best of

33 all._____ When I go up

37 yon - der_____ I'll al - ways re -

41 call_____ That old dus - ty

45 sad - dle_____ That hangs on the wall._____

His face was worn and wrinkled, his hair had turned to gray
He was an old time cowhand, that lived in yesterday,
He said he had a treasure he'd keep until he died,
And when I asked him what it was this old cowhand replied.

Chorus:
There's an old dusty saddle
That hangs on the wall
It's covered with memories
That I love best of all.
When I go up yonder
I'll always recall
that old dusty saddle
That hangs on the wall.

And as he told his story, My eyes filled up with tears
His heart was full of mem'ries, that lived down through the years,
I never will forget him, he treated me so kind,
And I still have the treasures of that dear old dad of mine.

Chorus

63

Bad Brahma Bull

Written by Curley Fletcher (composer of STRAWBERRY ROAN) in 1942.

Moderato

Words and Music by: Curley Fletcher

slow,   and   you   might   do   some   good   at   the   big   Ro - de -

o",   2.So   I

So I wraps up my riggin' and starts raisin' dust,
I'm huntin' that show and that brahma to bust,
So I enters that contest and pays entrance fee,
And tells them to look at the champion, that's me,
Well they look me all over and thinks that I'm full,
So they offers a seat on that bad brahma bull.
Sez I good enough 'cause I ain't here to brag
But I came a long ways just to gentle that stag.

Lay off the hard liquor and don't you get full
And think you can tame that there bad brahma bull,
Go right down and choose him and when you get through,
Just tell them you learned on the old Flyin' U.
You claim he's a bad one I guess he may be,
He looks like a sucklin' or weaner to me,
Go bring on your longhorn you never had one,
Could set me to guessin' nor bother me none.

So while they're a puttin' that bull in the chutes,
I'm a strappin' my spurs, to the heels of my boots,
I looks that bull over, and to my surprise,
It's a foot and a half, in between his two eyes.
Right on top of his shoulders, he got a big hump,
And I cinches my riggin', just back of that lump,
I lights in his saddle, and I lets out a scream,
He comes out with a beller, and the rest is a dream.

Well he jumps to the left, but he lands tow'rd the right,
But I ain't no green horn, I'm still sittin' tight,
The dust starts to foggin ' right out of his skin,
And he's a wavin' his horns, right under my chin.
At a sunnin' his belly, he couldn't be beat,
He's a showin' the buzzards, the soles of his feet,
He's a dippin' so low, that my boots fill with dirt,
And he's makin' a whip, of the tail of my shirt.

He's a snappin' the buttons, right off of my clothes,
Just a buckin' and bawlin' and a blowin' his nose,
The crowd was a cheerin' both me and that bull,
But he needed no help, while I had my hands full.
Then he goes to fence-rowin' and weavin' behind,
My heads starts to snappin' and I sorta went blind,
When he starts in high divin', I lets out a groan,
Next we went up together, but he comes back alone.

Up high I turns over, and below I kin see,
He's a pawin' up dirt, just a waitin' for me,
I can picture a grave, and a big slab of wood,
Readin' here lays the twister, that thought he was good,
Then I notices somethin' don't seem kin be true,
But the brand on his hip, was a big Flyin' U.
When I landed he charged, but I got enough sense,
To outrun that bull, to a hole in the fence.

I dives through that hole, and I want you to know,
That I ain't goin' back, to no wild west show,
At a straddlin' them brahm'ers you can bet I'm all through
And I'm a sore-footin' back, to the old Flyin' U.

Washtub Jerry (Jerry Wiant)

Bring Him Back Dead or Alive

The sad ballad of a bandit, who unknowingly shoots and kills his own brother; a sheriff who was hunting him down for his evil deeds.

Paul Kelso

Gan-non killed a man in Den-ton in the year of for-ty - five, Bring him back dead or a - live!_____ And the Sher-iff swore an oath on-ly one would sur-vive, He'd bring him back dead or a - live. Gan-non he was run-ning, he head-ed for Gaines - ville, Bring him back dead or a - live! Sher-iff swore to get him, "By God I will! I'll bring him back dead of a - live!"___ Gan-non on the cor-ner with a wild and fever-ish mind, Bring him back dead or a - live! He knew that the Sher-iff was not far be-hind, And he'd

66

bring him back dead or a - live, Bring him back dead or a - live!

—The Sher-iff cor-nered and he called him,— And Gan-non shot him down in the

streets,— Bring him back dead or a - live!— And

there he saw his broth-er, he was ly-ing at his feet, Bring him back dead or a -

live,— Bring him back dead or a - live, great God!

Bring him back dead or a - live!— "You can have my guns and horse and

I will sur-ren-der boys." Bring him back dead or a - live!— "If

you will hang me quick I'll es - cape my broth-er's voice!" Bring him back dead or a -

live,_____ Bring him back dead or a - live,_____

Bring him back dead or a - live!_____

1. Gannon killed a man in Denton in the year of forty-five,
Bring him back dead or alive!
And the sheriff swore an oath only one would survive,
He'd bring him back dead or alive.

2. Gannon he was running, he headed for Gainesville,
Bring him back dead or alive!
Sheriff swore to get him, "By God I will!
I'll bring him back dead or alive!"

3. Gannon on the corner with a wild and feverish mind,
Bring him back dead or alive!
He knew that the sheriff was not far behind,
And he'd bring him back dead or alive,
Bring him back dead or alive!

4. The sheriff cornered and he called him,
And Gannon shot him down in the streets,
Bring him back dead or alive!
And there he saw his brother, he was lying at his feet,
Bring him back dead or alive,
Bring him back dead or alive, great God!
Bring him back dead or alive!

5. "You can have my guns and horse and I will surrender, boys."
Bring him back dead or alive!
"If you will hang me quick I'll escape my brother's voice!"
Bring him back dead or alive,
Bring him back dead or alive,
Bring him back dead or alive!

Cowboy Tidbits

boar's nest
A cattle-ranch's *line camp.* Probably so called on account of the maleness of the occupants and the manner in which they kept house.

bob-tail guard
The first guard of the night on a trail-drive.

boot
(1) Originally a folding cover of leather or canvas on a gig or buggy, extending from the dashboard to the faces of passenger and driver, protecting them from rain and mud. The term also referred to the tarp or leather curtain used at the rear of a stagecoach to protect and retain baggage, and to the actual space for baggage and valuables in the front and rear of the coach.
(2) A horse-shoe with toe and heel calked to make it more solid.
(3) The scabbard or covering of a *saddle-gun* (rifle or carbine-more usually, the latter). Made of leather and carried on the saddle in a number of ways: it could be fastened under the girth and under the rider's leg, usually to the right; or it could hang by a loop from the saddlehorn, or by a single strap at the rear of the saddle.

boothill
Also known as the **boot graveyard.** The cemetery of a cow-town. The arguments over why it is so named will no doubt go on for some years yet. Certainly it is connected with a man's wish to die with his boots on. I don't doubt that at times men were bundled into their graves with their boots on, because it isn't easy to get a pair of boots off a stiff without damaging them. Also, many rough crosses over graves were decorated with the boots of the occupants.

border draw
A method of drawing a revolver with the weapon on the hip opposite the drawing hand, butt forward. Probably not the fastest way of drawing a gun, but many men favored it, especially when wearing a coat; also, for some, it was the best manner in which to wear and draw a gun on horseback. Though a cross- or side-draw would probably not have taken any longer than a regular draw with the earlier heavy, long-barreled guns of 1850-70, this was not the case with more modern revolvers and holsters designed for increasingly rapid removal of iron from leather.

-continued on page 88-

Buffalo Gals

This old song goes way back, back before the cowboy days with easy to remember words and melody it is well liked by everyone. By adding the official cowboy yodel (last two lines) makes this a traditional cowboy song

1. As I was walking down the street, down the street, down the street,
A pretty girl I chanced to meet ,
Under the silv'ry moon.

Chorus:
Buffalo gals won't you come out tonight, come out tonight, come out tonight,
Buffalo gals won't you come out tonight and dance by the light of the moon.

Yodel:
I ee-o lee ay lee-o lee-o lee ee lee-o lee ay lee-o ay lee lee-o lee
O ay lee-o lee la la la la la la O lee o lee-o lee ee

2. I asked her if she'd stop and talk, stop and talk, stop and talk,
Her feet covered up the whole sidewalk,
She was fair to view.

3. I ashed her if she'd be my wife, be my wife, be my wife,
Then I'd be happy all my life,
If she'd marry me.

69

By the Silv'ry Rio Grande

Traditional Cowboy Song

1. In the Lone Star State of Texas, by the silv'ry Rio Grande,
Strolled a couple one fine evening, two sweethearts hand in hand,
"Twas the ranchman's pretty daughter and the lad she loved so dear,
On the morrow they must part, for many a weary year.

Yodel:
O lee - o lee- o
lay layee - o lee - o - lee - ee

2. To Europe she was going, to become a lady grand,
Where her father hoped some earl or else count she'd wed,
She left the ranch next morning, tho' her heart was true to Jack,
Only yesterday a letter came, and this is what it said.
Yodel:

3. My heart's tonight in Texas, tho' I'm far across the sea,
For the band is playing Dixie, and it's there I long to be,
Dad says some earl I'll marry, but you shall have my hand,
For my heart's tonight in Texas, by the silv'ry Rio Grande.
Yodel:

4. In a stately hall in England stood the Texzs girl one night,
The scene was one of splendor and the lights were burning bright,
Before her knelt an earl, humbly begging for her hand,
But her thoughts were back in Texas, by the silv'ry Rio Grande.
Yodel:

5. "I can't say yes," she answered, "Your title cannot take,
There's a lad away in Texas, they call him Texas Jake,
It is long ago I promised, that dear Texas lad to wed,
Only yesterday I wrote, and it is thus the letter read."
Yodel:

6. "My heart's tonight in Texas, tho' I'm far across the sea,
Where the band is playing Dixie, and it's there I long to be,
Dad says some earl I'll marry, but you shall have my hand,
For my heart's tonight in Texas by the silv'ry Rio Grande."
Yodel:

Cheyenne
(Shy Ann)

Words by: Harry Williams
Music by: Egbert Van Alstyne

Composed in 1905 by Williams and Van Alstyne, this is probably the first hit cowboy song published in the USA. It was recorded in 1906 by Billy Murray.

Moderately Fast

Way out in old Wy - o - ming long a - go,
They rode that night and near - ly half the

go, Where coy - otes lurk while night winds howl and blow,
day, Chey - enne was six - ty sev - en mile a - way,

A cow - boys lus - ty voice rang out "Hel - lo!" And
But when at last they gal - loped up the street. The

ech - oed thro' the val - ley down be - low, Then came back a
cow - boy's pride was real - ly hard to beat, On his arm his

maid - en's an - swer sweet and clear, Cow - boy tossed his hat up in the
fu - ture bride a - car - ry - ing, But be - neath the lit - tle church - es

air, Said he, "I've come to take you right a - way from here,
dome, Said she, "I feel like turn - ing back, not mar - ry - ing,

71

Chey - enne, they say, is miles a - way but they've a preach - er there," Then
His face got red, and then he said, "You will or you'll walk home, If

she just drooped her eye, She was so ver - y shy, So shy oh my, and
you ride back to - day, You'll hon - or and o - bey," I do, I do, then

then he made re - ply, Oh! Oh! Oh!
he was heard to say, Oh! Oh! Oh!

The Nickel Creek Band
Sean Watkins, Sara Watkins, Chris Thile, and Scott Thile on stand up bass

Cowboy Boasters

Moderato

Cowboy Song

I'm a howl-er from the prai-ries of the West.___ If you
want to die with ter-ror look at me.___ I'm chain light-ning, If I
ain't, may I be blessed,___ I'm the snor-ter of the bound-less prai -
rie.___ He's a kill-er and a hat-er! He's the great an-ni-hi -
la-tor! He's a ter-ror of the bound-less prai - rie.___ He's a
kill-er and a hat-er! He's the great an-ni-hi-la-tor! He's the ter-ror of the
bound-less prai - rie.___

I'm the snoozer from the steepest upper trail!
I'm the reveler in murder and in gore!
I can bust more Pullman coaches on the rail -
Than anybody who has worked the job before.

He's a snorter and a snoozer!
He's the great trunk line abuser!
He's the man who puts the sleeper on the rail.

I'm the double-jawed hyena from the East.
I'm the blazing bloody blizzard of the States.
I'm the celebrated slugger; I'm the Beast -
I can snatch a man bald-headed while he waits.

He's a double-jawed hyena!
He's the villain of the scena!
He can snatch a man bald-headed while he waits.

Cowboy Jack

Another song from Arizona, the composer of Cowboy Jack is unknown. It was first published in 1928 and was made popular by the Carter Family in 1934. It remains one of the most popular of all cowboy folksongs.

Old Cowboy Tune

He was just a lone - ly cow - boy,_____ with a
They had learned to love each oth - er,_____ and had
He_____ joined a band of cow - boys,_____ and_____

heart so brave and true,_____ and he learned to
nam - ed their wed - ding day,_____ when a quar - rel
tried to for - get her name,_____ but_____ out on the

love a maid - en_____ with eyes of heav'ns own blue._____
come be - tween them,_____ and Jack he rode a - way._____
lone - ly prai - rie_____ she waits for him the same._____

He was just a lonely cowboy,
With a heart so brave and true,
And he learned to love a maiden,
With eyes of heav'n's own blue.

They had learned to love each other,
And had named their wedding day,
When a quarrel come between them,
And Jack he rode away.

He joined a band of cowboys,
And tried to forget her name,
but out on the lonely prairie,
She waits for him the same.

One night when work was finished,
Just at the close of day,
Some one said, "Sing a song Jack,"
"twill drive dull care away.

When Jack began his singing
His mind it wandered back,
For he sang of a maiden,
Who waited for her Jack.

"Out on the lonely prairie,
Where the skies are always blue,
Your sweetheart waits for you Jack,
Your sweetheart waits for you."

Jack left the camp next morning,
Breathing his sweethearts name,
"I'll go and ask forgiveness,
For I know I'm to blame.

But when he reached the prairies,
He found a new made mound,
And his friends they sadly told him,
They'd laid his loved one down.

They said as she was dying,
She breathed her sweetheart's name,
And asked them with her last breath,
To tell him when he came.

Your sweethearts waits for you Jack,
Your sweetheart waits for you,
Out on the lonely prairie,
Where the skies are always blue.

Cowboy's Dance Song

Lively

You ___ can't ex - pect a cow-boy to ag - i - tate his

shanks; In a et - i - quet - tish man - ner in ar - is - to - crat - ic

ranks, When he's al - ways been ac - cus - tomed to shake the heel and

toe, At the rat - tling ranch - er danc - es where much et - i - quette don't

go, You can bet I set them laugh - ing in quite an ex - cited

way; A giv - in' of their squin - ters an as - ton - ished sort of

play, When I hap - pened in - to Den - ver and was asked to take a

prance, In the smooth and eas - y maz - es, of a high toned dance.

Dusty Desert Trail

Lyric by: W. A. Thomas
Music by: Arthur Utt
and "Pappy" Cheshire

Dust - y Saddle I'm a rid - in' all day long; The winds are hot and burn - in' but my heart it sings a song. Wear - y cat - tle, old Pin - to don't you sigh; There's rest and shade a wait - in' when the sun sets in the sky.

Chorus

O'er the DUST - Y DES - ERT TRAIL when the even - in' sun goes down A cool - in' breeze is blow - in' lit - tle dog - gies play - in' 'round When the sil - ver moon is low, Then the old hy - e - nas'

wail, The camp-fires' light is shin-in' o'er the DUST-Y DES-ERT

TRAIL; And in it's light I see a face who's smil-in' just for

me, And ev'-ry night she's in my dreams, with her I long to

be, For the Ranch Boss in the sky, Gave my love a gold-en

veil, And to-night she is watch-ing o'er the DUST-Y DES-ERT TRAIL.

Fair Lady of the Plains

Joan O'Bryant

♩ = 84

(Verse 1, under music)
I once knew a maid-en who lived on the plains, She helped me to herd cat-tle through slow, stead-y rains, She helped me one sea-son, one whole year's round-up, But she would drink red liq-uor from a cold bit-ter cup.

She would drink red liquor, that affects a man's soul,
But she was a fair maiden and as white as the snow.
I learned her the cow trade, the ranger's command,
I learned her to handle a six-shooter in right or left hand.

I learned her to handle a six-shooter and never to run,
Never fear danger while a bullet's in a gun.
We camped in a canyon in the fall of the year,
We camped in a canyon with a bunch of fat steers.

The Indians broke in on us at the dead hour of night,
She had rose from her warm bed a battle to fight.
Then out roared the thunder and down come the rain,
Along come a bullet and crushed out her brain.

Now arise all you cowboys, let's fight for our life
For these wretched redskins have murdered my wife.

78

I Leave My Troubles at the Old Corral

Words by: Mildred Dixon
Music by: Tom Baker

I love to roam where the cattle feed,
    to breathe the prairie air,
I love to gaze on the tumble weed,
    without a single care.

Chorus:
I leave my troubles at the old corral when I ride off alone down the trail,
I go where I please, free as the desert breeze, that brings me the coyotes wail,
I keep a steady pace with the wind in my face 'till I reach the great divide,
I leave my troubles at the old corral, when I saddle my pony and ride.

I love to watch while the sun goes down what beauty to behold,
When shadows fall then I know I've found contentment for my soul.

Chorus

79

I'm Longing For The Range

Words and Music by:
Claude L Bailey, Henry J. Sommers and
Minnie M. Kilmer

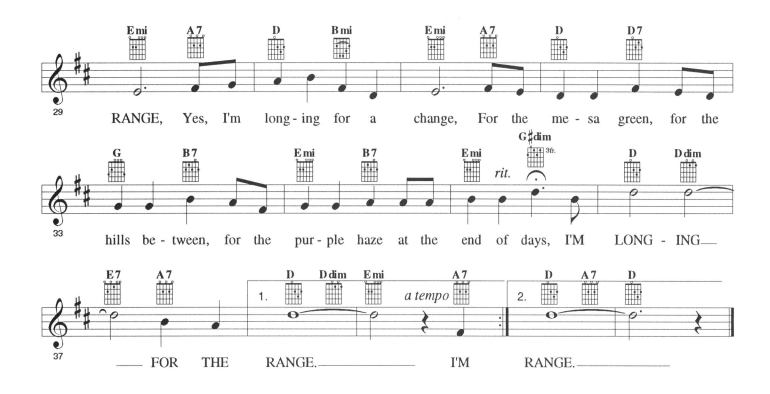

RANGE, Yes, I'm long-ing for a change, For the me-sa green, for the

hills be - tween, for the pur-ple haze at the end of days, I'M LONG - ING___

___ FOR THE RANGE.___ I'M RANGE.___

Cowgirls at Pendleton, Oregon, 1917
In 1911 one cowgirl at Pendleton came within two points of winning the All-Around
Championship, shortly thereafter cowgirls and cowboys competed separately.

I'm Trailing Back To You

Words and Music by:
Delores Dickens, Joseph Dobbs
and Ethel DePlanque

sun sets in the West, that's the time I love the best For it's then that I'm

trail - ing back to you   Whenthe   you.

Carl T. Sprague sang gen-
uine cowboy music in the
1920s and became known as
America's first singing cowboy. Carl's playing a very
early (1928) wood body
National Triolian guitar

Is The Range Still The Same Back Home?

Words and Music by:
(Red River) Dave Mc Enery

Moderately

D   **D7**   **G**

36   Home?_____ Has the West stood the test of time?_____

G mi   **D7**   **C#7**   **C7**   **B7**

41   ____ Oh, tell me, please do, I'm an old cow - boy too, Is The

A7   **D**   **D**   **G mi**   **D**

1.   2.

46   Range Still The Same Back Home?_____ Is The   Home?_____

"Red River" Dave
and his
Troubadours at the
New York World's Fair, 1939.
Red plays a rare Gibson style "O" guitar

"RED RIVER" DAVE and his TROUBADOURS, at the N.Y. WORLD'S FAIR — 1939.

Jim Oxford and His Salt Creek Girl

Moderato

Words by: J Frank Dobie

Well— I'm a bold cow-boy, from— Salt Creek I came; While—

vir - tue de - part - ed, a - las I pro - fane. In the cold ports of—

Cu - ba I'm— ve - ry well known As a rov - ing young cow - boy and

Bee - villes' my home.

1. While I'm a bold cowboy, from Salt Creek I came;
While virtue departed, alas I profane.
In the cold ports of Cuba I'm very well known
As a roving young cowboy and Beeville's my home.

2. I'll tell you my troubles without further delay,
How a pretty young lassie my heart stole away.
She was a farmer's daughter on the Salt Creek side,
And I always intended to make her my bride.

3. I worked for Wood and Kennedent, and earned quite a stake,
I stood fast and steady and never played nor drank.
I sent Emma my wages, the same to keep safe,
I begrudged her nothing that I had on earth.

4. One bright Sabbath morning a letter I received:
She said from her promise she long had been relieved.
And had married another, she long had delayed,
And the next time I saw her, she'd ne'er be a maid.

5. It's down on old Salt Creek for me there's no rest;
I'll saddle old Joe and I'll pull father west.
I'll go through Muskogee some good times to find,
And leave my old sweetheart with another behind.

6. Come, all ye bold cowboys, to you I'll tell true:
Don't depend on a woman, 'cause you're beat when you do.
But if ever you see one with a dark auburn curl,
Remember Jim Oxford and the Salt Creek girl.

Laramie Michael Malone

Moderate Waltz

by: William Allison

Oh, I'm a young poke who has wander-ed a - round thru our great wes - tern states—— I rode all a - lone. No hal - ter was known—— to me or my roan 'Till I land - ed in Lar - a - mie Town.—— 'Twas here that I met Kate the daugh - ter of one Who lived on raw whis - key and fought with a gun And he was a - swear - in', fight-in' son of a gun, Was Lar - a - mie Mich - ael Ma - lone.—— He fought for re - venge or he fought just for fun, He'd fight with his fists, a knife or a gun, He was - 'nt a -

fraid of the Dev-il's own son, That Lar-a-mie Mich-ael Ma-lone—

— He'd give an-y guy— the shirt off his back and when he got

drunk he would go take it back, Of ex-cite-ment a-round him there nev-er was a

lack, Tough Lar-a-mie Mich-ael Ma-lone.———————— I

I called on his daughter one day to propose
I thought I was handsome in my store-bought clothes.
But he just stood there a holdin' his nose,
That Laramie Michael Malone.
He only laughed when I asked to see Kate,
"N said in that get-up I'd sure get the gate,
"Twas that very moment I started to hate
Tough Laramie Michael Malone.
I said you laughin' hyena you think it's a joke,
Making fun of a poor lonesome cowpoke,
If you wasn't her pa your nose I would poke,
Laramie Michael Malone.
"Don't let that stop you, me fine buckaroo,"
Then he grabbed my left ear and started to chew,
"Twas like fightin' a bucksaw I suddenly knew,
Fightin' Laramie Michael Malone.

We fought for an hour we both were a sight,
And I thought that I was a winin' the fight
When all of a sudden I went out like a light,
Knocked out by Michael Malone.
When I came to I lay in Kate's bed,
She with a towel was bathin' my head,
In shame then I really wished I was dead,
Beaten by Michael Malone.
But Kate enderly kissed me and said tho' a sight
In a very short time that I'd be alright,
And that daddy was sorry that I had to fight
Tough Laramie Michael Malone.
Soon Kate and I married and in time had a son
Who turned out to be a fightin' son-of-a-gun,
In fact he was really just like the one
Called Laramie Michael Malone.

Cowboy Tidbits

border shift
The passing of a gun from one hand to the other during a gun-fight. Some men were said to be adept at this and could apparently do it without any break in their firing. If a man were right-handed and wounded in the right arm, he might pass his gun to his left hand; or, more rarely, he might be a two-gun man and, with both guns drawn, empty his right-hand gun and pass his left-hand gun into his right hand.
When "Long-haired" Jim Courtright, gun in hand, was shot in the gun-hand thumb by the little gamecock Luke Short, it is said that Jim tried the border shift - one of those tales that can never be proved, for before he could catch the gun in his right hand Luke had killed him. (Cunningham 1934; Ramon Adams 1944). Rossi 1975 shares my skepticism: "Seen more in Hollywood and Western fiction than in real life. If Courtright tried the trick in this serious predicament, he deserved to get shot. Folks said he tried the border shift and the story grew."

boss
(1) As **Boss**, a term for the buffalo, used in the early days. Possibly from the Latin *bos,* the generic name for cattle.
(2) **Boss of the Plains** shortened to **Boss**, which John B. Stetson first called the famous hat he designed for the cattleman. The name did not catch on and the hat survived to be called the **John B. Stetson,** the **Stetson,** or simply the **JB** or the **JohnB.**

bottom
(1) Low-lying land, particularly that with water lying on it or flowing through it. Also **bottom lands.**
(2) The stamina or staying power of a horse. A horse with it was said to have **plenty of bottom.**

Brahma cattle
Also **Brahman cattle, zebu.** The Longhorns did not carry enough beef in Texas. When they were crossed with Durhams and Herefords, the offspring put on the beef, but were not immune like the Longhorn, to **Texas fever.** Descendants of the Asian-Indian Brahma stock, which had been introduced into South Carolina in 1849, were experimented with on the great King Ranch. They came into Texas in the early 1880's to be retained "in breed," but also to cross with Longhorns and Longhorn-shorthorn crosses. Though they were better able to survive Texas fever than were the shorthorns, they did not have the hardiness associated with the Longhorns.

-continued on page 105-

La Vaquilla Colorada
(The Little Red Heifer)

This is a well known *corrido* (topical, narrative ballad) is said to be from Sonora, Mexico. It tells about a reluctant heifer and the problems she causes the cowboys. The cowboys finally have to use a sharp prod to get her in the pen. *Vaqueros* used *garrochas*, or prods, until the middle of the 19th Century when roping took over as the preferred manner of cattle management

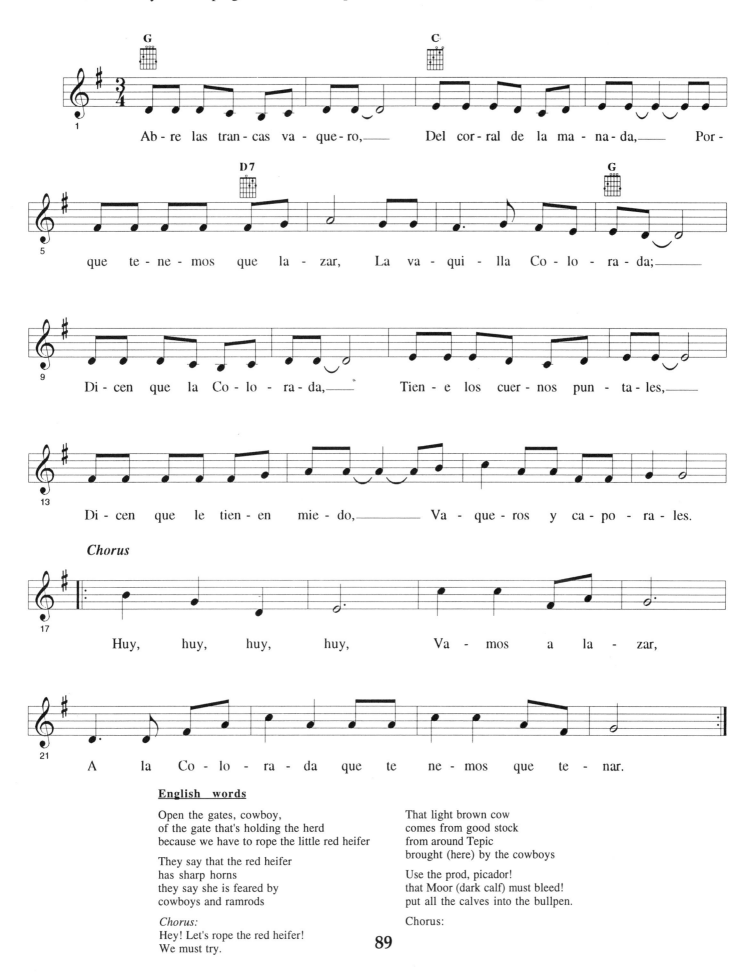

English words

Open the gates, cowboy,
of the gate that's holding the herd
because we have to rope the little red heifer

They say that the red heifer
has sharp horns
they say she is feared by
cowboys and ramrods

Chorus:
Hey! Let's rope the red heifer!
We must try.

That light brown cow
comes from good stock
from around Tepic
brought (here) by the cowboys

Use the prod, picador!
that Moor (dark calf) must bleed!
put all the calves into the bullpen.

Chorus:

Little Joe, The Wrangler's Sister Nell

This song is usually attributed to Jack Thorpe, the composer of LITTLE JOE THE WRANGLER. It may well be by Thorpe but he never admitted or denied his contribution.

Moderato

Words by: N. Howard (Jack Thorp)

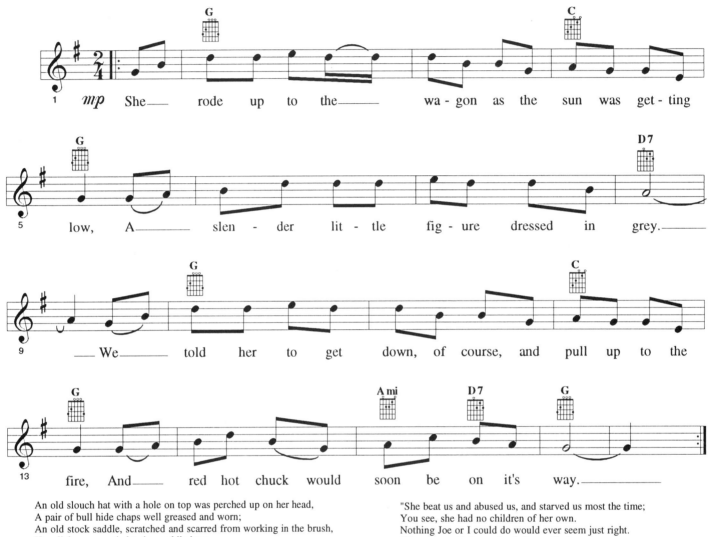

An old slouch hat with a hole on top was perched up on her head,
A pair of bull hide chaps well greased and worn;
An old stock saddle, scratched and scarred from working in the brush,
Her slick maguey tied to her saddle horn.

She said she rode from Llano, four hundred miles away;
Her pony was so tired it couldn't go.
She asked to stop a day or two and kind of rest him up;
Then maybe she could find her brother Joe.

We could see that she'd been crying, her little face was sad;
When she spoke, her upper lip would tremble so.
She was the living image, we all saw at a glance,
Of our little, lost horse-herder, Wrangler Joe.

We asked where Joe was working, if she knew the outfit's brand;
Yes, his letter said it was the Circle Bar.
It was mailed at Amarillo about three months ago,
From a trail herd headed north to Cinnabar.

I looked at Jim, he looked at Tom, and then looked back at me;
There was something in our hearts, we couldn't speak.
She said she got kind of worried when whe never heard no more,
And things at home got tougher every week.

"You see, my mother died," she said, "when Joe and I was born,
So Joe and I was twins", her story ran;
"Then Dad, he ups and marries, and gets another wife,
And then it was our troubles sure began.

"She beat us and abused us, and starved us most the time;
You see, she had no children of her own.
Nothing Joe or I could do would ever seem just right.
When Joe pulled out, that left me all alone."

I gave the kid my bed-roll, while I bunked in with Jim;
We talked and planned and schemed the whole night through,
As to which of us would tell her the way that Joe was killed,
And break the news as gently as we knew.

"I'll wrangle in the morning, boys," she said as she turned in,
"I'll have the horses at the wagon 'fore it's day."
As the morning star was rising, I saw the kid roll out,
Saddle up the gray night-horse and ride away.

Soon we heard the horses coming, a-headed into camp.
It wasn't light we could plainly hear the bell,
And then someone a-crying, a-coming on behind,
"Twas Little Joe the Wrangler's Sister Nell.

We couldn't quite console her, she'd seen the horses' brands,
As she drove them from the river's bank below;
From the look on our faces she seemed to realize
That she ne'er again would see poor Wrangler Joe.

Make Me a Cowboy Again

1. Backward, turn backward, oh, time on your wheels,
Airplanes and wagons and automobiles,
Dress me once more in sombrero that flaps,
Spurs, flannel shirt, boots, slicker and chaps.
Give me a six shooter or two in my hand;
Show me a steer to rope and to brand;
Out where the sage brush is dusty and gray,
Make me a cowboy again for a day.

2. Give me a broncho that knows how to dance,
Buckskin of color and wicked of glance;
New to the feeling of bridle and bits.
Give me a quirt that will sting when it hits.
Strap on a poncho behind in my roll;
Pass me the lariat so dear to my soul.
Over the trail let me lope far away.
Make me a cowboy again for a day.

3. Thunder of hoofs over range as we ride,
Hissing of iron and smoking of hide
Bellow of cattle and snort of cayuse,
Longhorns from Texas as wild as the deuce;
Midnight stampedes and milling of herds.
Yells from the cowmen, too angry for words;
Right in the midst of it all would I stay:
Make me a cowboy again for a day.

4. Under the star-studded canopy vast,
Camp-fire, coffee and comfort at last.
Tales of the ranchmen and rustlers re-told,
Over the pipes as the embers grow cold.
These are the tunes that old memories play;
Make me a cowboy again for a day.
(repeat last two lines)

Mexicali Rose

This song was composed by bandleader Jack Tenney in 1923. Following its publication in 1935, this song was recorded by many artists including Roy Rogers and Bob Wills.

Music by: Jack B. Tenney
Words by: Helen Stone

Tempo Di Tempo

pin - ing, Ev - 'ry hour a year while I'm a - way,_____

Dry those big brown eyes and smile, dear, Ban - ish all those tears and please don't

sigh._____ Kiss me once a - gain and hold me;

Mex - i - cal - i Rose good - bye.   bye._____

1. Mexicali Rose, I'm leaving, don't feel blue.
Mexicali Rose, stop grieving; I love you.
When the dove of love is winging thru the blue,
All the castles you've been building will come true.

Chorus:
Mexicali Rose, stop crying;
  I'll come back to you some sunny day.
Ev'ry night you'll know that I'll be pinning,
  Ev'ry hour a year while I'm away,
Dry those big brown eyes and smile, dear,
  bannish all those tears and please don't sigh.
Kiss me once again and hold me; Mexicali Rose good-bye.

2. Mexicali Rose, I'll miss you when I go.
There'll be times I'll long to kiss you, that I know.
All the while I'll just be yearning, lonesome too,
Counting days 'till I'm returning, dear, to you.

Chorus

Saloon Smashed, Husband Bashed

   Friday last, chaos arrived at the Deadwood Saloon in the form of
Pearl and Dan Hart.

   The evening's events began with a march of the Deadwood Ladies
Temperance League, led by Pearl Hart, to the establishment where Dan
Hart was participating in Friday Night Poker Club festivities without
spousal consent.

   "We shall come face-to-face with degradation," she promised her
followers. However, when the first face she found at the saloon
belonged to her dearly betrothed, the march became a massacre.

   His thought process clouded by a two pair of nines, Dan Hart did not
grasp the wholeness of his peril at first. It took a second glance into
the fires of Pearl's eyes to topple his chair backwards and send the best
poker hand of his life flying.

   Before the cards hit the floor, Pearl had commenced to swat his sins
away with the "Down with the Demon Rum" placard she had carried.
As Dan fled from the room, the errant swings from her staff of
abstinence swept fourteen bottles of *Ol' Rub of the Brush* onto the floor.

   Miss Belle, Proprietress of the saloon, declined to seek any
compensation for the lost whiskey. "After all," she said, "on a good
night, Dan spills more than that."

My Ma Was Born In Texas

A cowboy's life, of truth and lies. The choices he made and his timely good-byes.

Cowboy Song

My Ma was born in Tex - as, my Pa in Ten - nes - see, They were mar - ried in the sum - mer of eigh - teen nine - ty three. They moved to Cal - i - for - ni - a and that's where I was born, In a roll - in' cov - ered wag - on on a bright Sep - tem - ber

1. G

last time

morn.   wife.

"Some of my experiences were going hungry, getting wet and cold, riding sorebacked horses, going to sleep on herd and loosing cattle, getting cussed by the boss, scouting for gray-backs (body lice), trying the sick racket now and then to get a night's sleep. . . but all of these things were forgotten when we delivered the herd and started back to grand old Texas. . . I always had the "big time" when I arrived in San Antonio rigged out with a pair of high-heeled boots and striped pants and about $6.30 worth of other clothes. This "big time" would last but a few days, however, for I would soon be busted and have to borrow money to get out to the ranch, where I would put in the fall and winter telling about the big things I had seen up North. The next spring I would have the same old trip, the same old things would happen in the same old way, and with the same old wind-up. I put in eighteen or twenty years on the trail and all I had in the final outcome was the high-heeled boots, the striped pants and about $4.80 worth of other clothes, so there you are"

G. O. Burrows former cowboy of Del Rio, Texas

1. My ma was born in Texas, my pa in Tennessee,
They were married in the summer of eighteen ninety-three
They moved to California and that's where I was born,
In a rollin' covered wagon on a bright September morn.

2. I grew up in my saddle, my play toy was a gun,
Shooting at the rattlesnakes was my idea of fun.
"Twas at the age of seventeen I left my happy home,
The open range was calling and my time had come to roam.

3. I met a fair young maiden, she's the flower of the plains,
I married her one morning, which showed I had no brains.
She said she was a maiden, but oh, how she had lied,
When the honeymoon was over, seven kids were by her side.

4. Oh, I was disappointed, but I said I didn't mind,
I remained her husband, honest, true and kind,
Until one night I found her upon a stranger's knee,
To be her long-lost cousin he was introduced to me.

5. I knew that she was lying, so I pulled my gun and said,
"You're a low down, sneakin' coward," and I filled him full of lead.
The jury found me guilty and they sentenced me for life,
But I'm better off in prison than to live with such a wife.

Sons Of The Pioneers c.1940
front row: Bob Nolan, Lloyd Perryman, Hugh Farr
back row: Tim Spencer, Karl Farr, Pat Brady
Lloyd playing a rare Larson's brothers guitar

Photo courtesy L. L. Griffin

Pfeiffer Brothers

TIP TOP

SONGS of the ROAMING RANGER
50
FAVORITE & ORIGINAL
COW BOY SONGS and
MOUNTAIN BALLADS.
Complete with Guitar and Ukulele Chords.

A PART OF THE CONTENTS: ROAMING RANGER • PRAIRIE YODEL BLUES
MY ROCKY MOUNTAIN HOME • IN 1895 • THE WEEKS GO INTO MONTHS
THE WYOMING TRAIL • DON'T HANG ME IN THE MORNIN'
THE COWMAN'S PRAYER • IN THE VALLEY OF YESTERDAY
MY HOME IN OKLAHOMA ....AND 40 OTHER PLEASING SONGS

Old Timer

The retirement of an old buckaroo, his time has come to rest;
His pony's tired, his gear is worn, but he always did his best.

Words by: Ike Griffith
Music by: Jack Cranford

Chord symbols above measure 29: C, C°, C, G7

29 rop - in the stray to brand, With time to spare for herd - ing steers,

Chord symbols above measure 33: C, D7, G7, G aug, C, G aug, C, C7

33 o - ver th roll - ing sand, Your pin - to is lame and wear - y, his

Chord symbols above measure 37: F, C, G7, C, G7, C, G7, C, G7

37 round - up days are through, Good - bye to your old pal, he'll stay in the cor - ral, Old

Chord symbols above measure 41: C, F mi7, G7, C

41 Tim - er, old buck - a - roo.

**Jimmy Wakely with Mary Ford, plus
Johnny Bond hanging on to that Gibson tenor banjo**
Jimmy Wakely was called "The Melody Kid," in movies,
Johnny Bond wrote the standard song *Cimarron,*
Mary Ford became the better half of Les Paul

Only A Lonesome Cowboy

Music and Lyrics by:
Vera Thompson Ross
Florence L. Yarwood
& Truscott Van Fossen

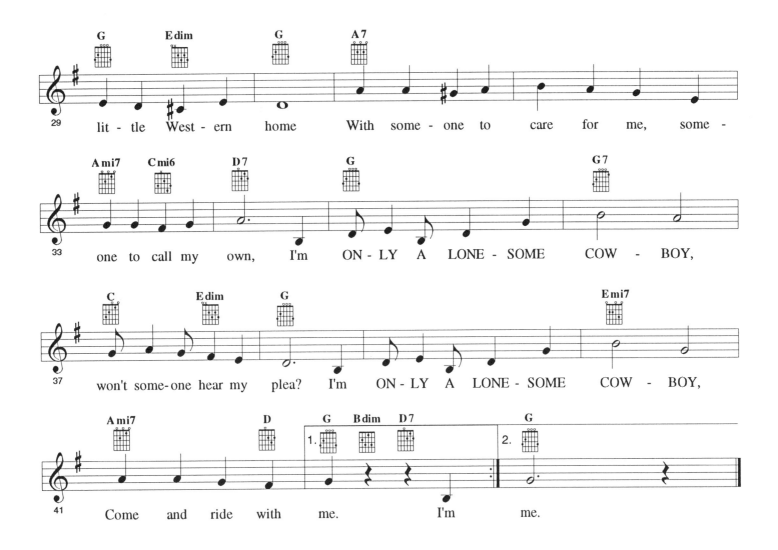

This cowboy's life is dreary, I'm weary of the range,
With no one dear to cheer me I'm longing for a change;

Refrain:
I'm only a lonesome cowboy, ridin' the range all day,
I'm only a lonesome cowboy, ridin' my life away,
Over the plains I wander, singing a plaintive song,
Countin' the days I squander, just lopin' along;
How I long to settle down in a little Western home
With someone to care for me, someone to call my own,
I'm only a lonesome cowboy, won't someone hear my plea?
I'm only a lonesome cowboy, come and ride with me.

Renate and Jim Easterbrook

TUMBLING TUMBLEWEEDS
or The American West Rolls On

See them tumbling down,
Pledging their love to the ground,
Lonely but free I'll be found,
Drifting along with the tumbling tumbleweeds.
--"Tumbling Tumbleweeds, " Bob Nolan

"Tumbling Tumbleweeds" was recorded in 1934 by the Sons of the Pioneers; and Bob Nolan, the composer, was not the only one who believed tumbleweeds to be a western symbol.

Actually, tumbleweeds originally came from Russia. They were transported here with flax seed which was imported by the Ukrainian farmers. And first appeared in South Dakota around 1877.

Tumbleweed is the common name for any usually globular plant in which the stem snaps off at ground level and the above ground portion is rolled and tumbled along by the wind, thereby scattering the seeds.

At first it was only a local problem but by 1881, tumbleweeds had blown across the northern Great Plains. Many farms and fields were over run by the fast-growing weed, with spines capable of tearing the flesh of horses and humans. and was such a problem that it came to the attention of the Secretary of Agriculture James Rusk to see what could be done. One idea (proposed by a state legislator) was to put a wire fence around the whole North Dakota state. Tumbleweeds continued to travel from farm to farm through the seeds that were carried unknowingly in the farm equipment, and through grain shipments by the railroad, spreading the weed further west.

To the immigrants, tumbleweed was called "Wind Witch" and "Leap the Field" because it was highly flammable, a burning tumbleweed could spread prairie fires by rolling and tumbling along with the wind across the fields, burning houses and crops. The Hopi Indians called it "white man's plant,"

After spring and summer rains, the bright green plants sprouted through the bare ground. Tiny green flowers bloom at the base of the leaves at about two months old. As the tumbleweed sheds its leaves, the seeds form and ripen. The tumbleweed plant becomes a dry, spiny globular mass that forms in various sizes.

Most seeds sprout by cell division, growing cell by cell, but not tumbleweed. Since tumbleweed's seeds already contain the infant plant, coiled up as tight as an mean rattler, germination is a matter of simply uncoiling. If the root finds enough moisture, the two slender, needle like seed leaves spread out and the seedling is off and growing. During the droughts in the 1930's farmers fed the young tumbleweed shoots to their starving livestock. But all to quickly, the fast-growing plant becomes inedible because of its tough and prickly stems.

In the autumn, the stem breaks off and the tumbleweed rolls and tumbles with the wind across fields or prairies spreading its seeds. A single plant can produce up to 250,000 seeds.

By now tumbleweeds seemed to appear everywhere, in fields, farms, prairies, rangelands, along the railways and road sides.

The best known tumbleweeds of the U.S. are the bugweed, *Corispermum hyssopifolium;* the Russian thistle, *Salsola kali,* naturalized in the U.S. from Asia and the tumbling pigweed, *Amaranthus retroflexus.*

Today, the tumbleweed has become a familiar part of our Western landscape, and the rollin,' rollin' tumbleweed symbolizes a part of Western myth and legend.

Over the Tumbleweed Trail

Words by: Kathryn F. Cochran
Music by: J.E. Robinson

At the close of the day when the stars light the way——— And the

moon - light is sil - ve - ry pale,——— Then the feet of my horse take the

hap - pi - est course Ov - er the tum - ble - weed trail. To a

ranch house that lies in the val - ley In a group of old cot - ton wood

trees, And a sweet - heart that waits in the moon - light with a

heart that beats on - ly for me. At the set of the sun, When the

long day is done—— And the night air is cool - ing and sweet——— Then we'll

haste to her side my—— po - ny and I to lay our two hearts at her

feet, For her pro - mise at last has been giv - en to me—— and

that is the end of the tale—— I am rid - ing my way in - to

hea - ven to - day Ov - er the Tum - ble - weed trail.

Pride of the Prairie

Composed in 1907 by Brenn and Botsford, this vaudeville tune became popular on both sides of the Atlantic.

Music by: George Botsford
Words by: Henry J. Breen

Allegro Moderato

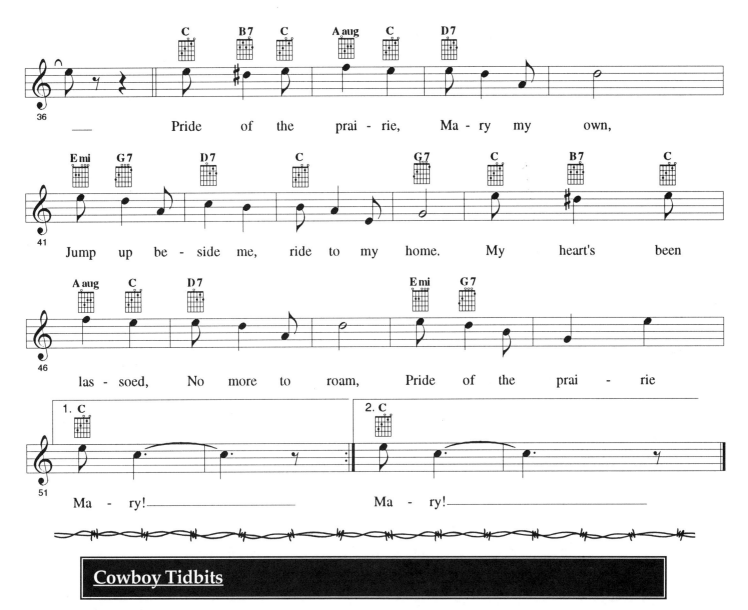

Pride of the prai - rie, Ma - ry my own,

Jump up be - side me, ride to my home. My heart's been

las - soed, No more to roam, Pride of the prai - rie

Ma - ry! Ma - ry!

Cowboy Tidbits

brand blotter

Also **brand blocher**, **brand blotcher**, A man who blotted out brands with further burning to destroy the identity of the cattle, with a view to stealing them.

brand book

The use of brand books varied according to time and place, but, for example, in Montana and Wyoming in the 1880s a legal brand was obtained from and recorded by the county clerk and the list of brands was open to public inspection. Plainly, in the later days of the West the whole branding system was tightened up. In the earlier days, in Texas, the situation was freer, though brand records did exist.

brander

The man who, at branding time, actually applied the hot iron to the hide of the animal.

branding crew

Men of a cow-outfit detailed for the job of cutting out, roping, throwing, and branding cattle.

braned inspector

An inspector of brands hired by cattlemen's associations to check cow-stealing and the sale of stolen cattle.

brush-popper

Applied to both men and horses that popped or drove Longhorns from the dense thickets of the Texas **brasada.**

California banknote

A cowhide; used as currency in California before the goldrush of 1849.

California moccasins

Sacks tied around the feet as protection against extreme cold. You can imagine this being practiced on the old California Trail in the High Sierras.

California pants

Striped or checked pants of heavy wool, hard-wearing and favored for use on the range; this in spite of the current belief that all cattlemen wore Levi's.

chap guard

A small protuberance (a knob or hook) on the shank of a spur to prevent the chaps from catching on the rowel.

chapping

The beating of a man with *leggins.* This could be a serious punishment for a transgression by a member of a cow-crew or it could be carried out mildly in fun.

Charlie Taylor

A makeshift butter made of molasses and fat.

Cheyenne leg

Also **Cheyenne cut.** A modification of the *winged chaps* developed in Wyoming. It was cut away on the under part of the thigh and lacked fastening below the knee.

Cheyenne roll

A saddle with a leather flange extending, over, to the rear, of the cantle-board. It was originated by Frank Meanea, a saddlemaker from that town, and one of the greatest makers of Western saddles.

-continued on page 109-

Punchin' Dough

(A Cook's Song)

Tune: "The Railroad Song"
Words by: Henry Herbert Knibbs

Moderato

Come, all you young wad-dies, I'll sing you a song; Stand back from the wa-gon, stay where you be-long. I've heard you ob-serv-in' I'm fus-sy and slow, While you're punch-in' cat-tle and I'm punch-in' dough.

1. Come, all you young waddies, I'll sing you a song;
Stand back from the wagon, stay where you belong.
I've heard you observin' I'm fussy and slow,
While you're punchin' cattle and I'm punchin' dough.

2. Now, I reckon your stomach would grow to your back .
If it wasn't for the cook that keeps fillin' the slack,
With the beans in the box and the pork in the tub,
I'm a wonderin' now who would fill you with grub.

3. You think you're right handy with gun and with rope,
But I've noticed you're bashful when usin' the soap.
When you're rollin' your Bull for your brown cigarette,
I been rolin' the dough for them biscuits you et.

4. When you're cuttin'stock, then I'm cuttin' steak;
When you're wranglin' hosses, I'm wrangling a cake.
When you're hazin' the dogies and battin' your eyes,
I'm hazin' dried apples that aim to be pies.

5. You brag about shootin' up windows and lights,
but try shootin' biscuits for twelve appetites.
When you crawl from your roll and the ground, it is froze,
Then who biles the coffee that thaws out your nose?

6. In the old days the punchers took just what they got:
It was sow-belly, beans and the old coffee pot.
But now you come howlin' for pie and for cake,
Then you cuss at the cook for a good bellyache.

7. You say that I'm old with my feet on the skids,
Well, I'm tellin' you that you're nothin' but kids.
If you reckon your mounts are some snaky and raw,
Just try ridin' herd on a stove that won't draw.

8. When you look at my apron, you're readin' my brand,
Four-X, which is sign for the best in the land.
On bottle or sack it sure stands for good luck,
So line up you waddies, and wrangle your chuck.

9. No use of you snortin' and fightin' your head;
If you like it with chili, just eat what I said,
For I am the boss of this end of the show,
While you're punchin' cattle and I'm punchin' dough.

Red River Shore

A narrative song, "I met a fair maiden, the girl I adore," who lives beneath a mountain on the Red River Shore. Her father refuses her hand to the cowboy, who jumps on his bronco and rides away. But the sorrowing girl summons him back with a letter. By the time he reaches the Red River Shore, however, she has drowned herself in despair

♩ = 104

Cowboy Ballad

Unhurried, with sentiment

At the foot of yon mount-ain, where the fount-ain doth flow, The
I spoke to her kind-ly, say-ing "Will you mar-ry me? My

great-est cre - a-tion, where the soft winds doth blow, I met a fair
for-tune's not great."____ "No mat-ter," said she. "Your beau-ty's a

maid-en; she's the one I a - dore; She's the girl I will mar-ry on the
plen-ty, you're the one I a - dore; You're the girl I will mar-ry on the

Red Riv - er shore.
Red Riv - er shore."

Verse 3
I asked her old father, if he'd giver her to me.
"No sir, she shan't marry no cowboy," said he.
So I jumped on my bronco and away I did ride
A-leaving my true love on the Red River side

Verse 4
Her cruel old father did thus interfere,
Saying he would deprive her of the dearest so dear;
He would send him away where the cannon do roar
Away from his true love on the Red River shore.

Verse 5
She wrote me a letter, and she wrote it so kind,
And in this letter these words you could find:
"Come back to me darling: you're the one I adore.
You're the one I would marry on the Red River shore.

Verse 6
I read this letter through till it made my heart sad,
And none of the fellows could make my heart glad;
Now I'm not used to stoppin', and you may be sure,
I was bound for my true love on the Red River shore.

Verse 7
So I jumped on my bronco and away I did ride
To marry my true love on the Red River side.
But her dad knew the secret, and with twenty and four
Came to fight this young cowboy on the Red River shore.

Verse 8
I drew my six-shooter, spun around and around
Till six men sere wounded and seven were down.
No use for an army of twenty and four;
I'm bound for my true love on the Red River shore.

Verse 9
Such is the fortune of all womenkind,
They are always controlled, they are always made mind;
Controlled by their parents until they become wives,
And slaves of their husbands the rest of their lives.

Verse 10
Hard luck in this world for all womenkind;
To those who are single the world o'er I find-
Confined with their parent's until they are wives,
And stay with their husbands the rest of their lives

Red Wing

Published in 1907, this song was composed by Mills and Chattaway. Mills' music is based on a 1849 piece by Schumann. Many songs were written about romantizied Indians in the early 1900s. Red Wing became the most popular and the most parodied.

♩ = 90

Robert R. Lyman

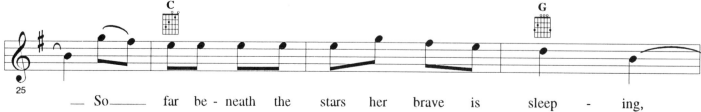

There once was an In - dian maid, A shy lit - tle prai - rie maid, She sang a - way a love song gay, As out on the prai - rie she whiled a - way the day. She loved a war - rior bold, This shy lit - tle maid of old. Brave and gay he rode one day To a bat - tle far a - way. Now the moon shines to - night on pret - ty Red Wing,— —The breez - es sigh - ing,— the night birds cry - ing.— — So — far be - neath the stars her brave is sleep - ing,

Chorus

108

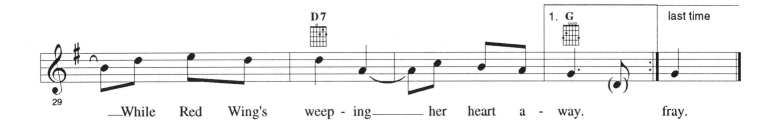

—While Red Wing's weep-ing——— her heart a - way.　　fray.

There once lived an Indian maid,
A shy little prairie maid,
She sang away a love song gay
As out on the prairie she whiled away the day.
She loved a warrior bold,
This shy little maid of old.
Brave and gay he rode one day
To a battle far away.

Chorus:

Now the moon shines tonight on pretty Red Wing,
The breezes sighing, the night birds crying.
So far beneath the stars her brave is sleeping,
While Red Wings's weeping her heart away.

She watched for him night and day
And kept all the campfires bright.
Each night she would lie in under the sky
And dream of his coming bye and bye.
When all the braves returned
The heart of Red Wing yearned,
Far, far way her warrior gay
Fell bravely in the fray.

No, this is not the face of Red Wing the shy little prairie maid, but it is **Red Cloud** (1822-1909). Chief of the Oglala tribe and leader of the fight against U.S. encroachment on Indian lands.

Cowboy Tidbits

chip box
Also **chip pile**. Where the buffalo or cowchip fuel was kept at a ranch or in camp.
chuck
Food, grub, chow.
chuck away
Meal-time, the cook's summons for the men to eat.
chuck box
The cook's hold-all box at the rear of the chuck wagon. It did not appear in the very early days of trail-driving and certainly not on the early Texas cowhunts, when not even chuck wagons were used, but developed in design as the northern drives became commonplace. The first chuck box was said to have been built into an ex-army wagon by Charles Goodnight of the Texas Rangers and the famous Goodnight Loving Trail - one of the greatest cowmen of them all.
chuck-line rider
Also **grub-line rider.** A man, out of work or just plain idle, who rode from ranch to ranch for free chuck or grub.
chuck wagon
The wagon that was a cookhouse on wheels for trail-drives and round-ups. Not employed during the early cowhunts in Texas, when every man was expected to carry his own grub, the chuck wagon was no more than an ordinary ranch-wagon, usually pulled by a pair of mules (or, in the early days, by a span of oxen), and with a box full of drawers and shelves at the tail-end. The men's personal gear might be carried in the bed of the wagon, and underneath would be slung the *cooney,* or cradle, for carrying various items, including wood or cowchips for fuel. The chuck wagon was the social center of the round-up and the meeting-place for any riders scattered on the trail-drive. Here the cook reigned supreme, and it was not only bad manners but imprudent either to raise dust near the cook's area or to help yourself to anything from his stores.
cimarrones
(Sp:wild ones). The wild black cattle of Texas. Often, however, the name was applied to intractable Longhorns, or men who stayed apart from the rest of their kind.
clear-footed
Said of a horse whose gait was clean and sure.
cocktail guard
Also **cocktail relief.** The last guard of the night on a trail-drive
Comancheros
Men, usually of Mexican-Indian hybrid origin, who might be called the go-betweens for the Comanche Indians and the whites. They were the trading link between the two peoples and were a natural development from the ciboleros. The Comanches would plunder in Old Mexico and sell through the Comancheros to the whites, and vice versa. Mostly by tacit consent, the Comancheros were neutral, because one party might gain and the other at least recoup losses by their existence. The Comancheros were also used in the release of white captives from the Indians, and needless to say, were neither admired nor loved by the Texans.

-continued on page 110-

Rodeo Days

Words by: S. Omar Baker
Music by: Kenneth S. Clark

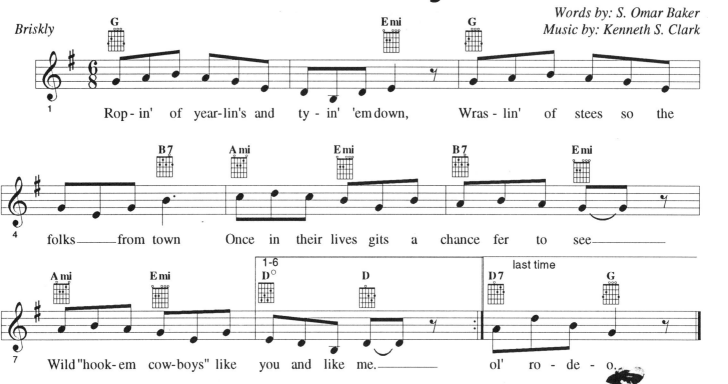

Briskly

G Rop-in' of year-lin's and ty-in' 'em down, **E mi** **G** Wras-lin' of stees so the

B 7 folks——from town **A mi** Once in their lives gits a **E mi** chance fer to see—— **B 7** **E mi**

A mi Wild "hook-em cow-boys" like **E mi** you and like me.—— **1-6 D°** **D** ol' ro-de-o. **last time D7** **G**

2. Stradlin' of broncos just out of the chutes,
Forkin' 'em bare-back like Injun Piutes,
Rakin' the shoulders of bellerin' steers;
Hearin' the audience whoopin' their cheers.

3. Milkin' wild cows and a ridin' wild mules,
Wearin' silk shirts an a yellin' like fools,
Cowboys is in from the ranches in dozens,
Whoopin' em up fer their city cousins.

4. Dancin' all night and a rainin' the deuce,
Millin' the streets like a loco cayuse;
Seems kinder funny fer us quiet boys
To raise so much rumpus and rouse so much noise!

5. Buckin' the contests we play at a battle,
Learned on the ranges a workin' with cattle.
What we put on ain't no circusy show
It's workaday stuff, this here wild rodeo!

6. Makin' a game of rough skill and of muscles,
Lettin' America witness our tussels,
Born of frontierin' and dear to the hearts
Of every old waddy in these western parts.

7. Rodeo time is fer rompin' and rarin',
Ridin' and ropin' and doin' yer darin',
They say the cowboy is doomed fer to go.
Hi-yip! We've still got the ol' rodeo.

Cowboy Tidbits

Comanche Trail
The trail from the Staked Plain down into Old Mexico which the Comanches took on their raids into that country.

contraries
Members of an Indian society, especially among the Sioux, who were the clowns and jesters of the tribe. Their specialty was to do anything backward: dress backward, walk backward, etc. They were greatly valued and treated with respect.

cooks
Though there was nothing romantic about a cook, and though he might be looked down on by the elevated horseman, he was respected, valued, and often feared. He was one of the unsung heroes of the West, and on him rested much of the morale of the outfit. A bad cook invariably spoiled a good crew and made an indifferent one bad. Fortunately for Western buffs, one or two excellent writers have given due credit and color to the breed who produced hot meals after hail-storms, stampedes, and day-long drives; who medicked the sick; and who, on more than one occasion, shot to death a man who broke the rule that nobody approached the chuck wagon without the cook's permission. Many were self-willed tyrants with the temperament of prima donna; many were the reason why good cowmen hired out to the brand that employed them.

corral
(Sp). A pen or enclosure to confine horses or cattle. Commonly in Western literature it was composed of posts and poles, but there were many varieties, including temporary corrals of rope; in the Southwest they were frequently made of high adobe walls to keep out marauding Indians.

coulee
(Fr *couler:* to flow; mainly NW) Also **cooley, coolly.** A steep-sided ravine, gully, or valley.

dally
To take a turn around the saddlehorn with a lasso after the throw had been made - as opposed to the hard-and-fast method in which the rope-end was permanently fastened to the horn. The dally man could, if necessary, ease off the rope to relieve the immense strain on it, essential sometimes with the rawhide reata, which could snap. Mexicans were dally men almost to a man

dally man
A man who threw a loose rope and tuned it around the saddlehorn after he had caught his animal; as opposed to a man who threw a fixed rope. It was said that if a man had a thumb missing, that was sure proof he was a dally man - which illustrates that if you weren't good at the art, you'd best not employ it at all, because you paid dearly for a mistake.

day wrangler
The remudero, or hand in charge of the remuda (horse-herd) by day as opposed to the night wrangler, or night-hawk, who had charge of it by night.

 -continued on page 113-

Roving Cowboy

♩ = 80

Buell Kazee

Lyrics (under the staff):

Come all you rov-ing cow-boys, bow down your head and hand, I'll tell to you a sto-ry while you a-round me stand. I'm goin' to quit this wild west, this bleak and storm-y plain, Where the In-dians prowl I'll leave you to ne'er re-turn a-gain.

1. Come all you roving cowboys, bow down your head and hand,
I'll tell to you a story while you around me stand.
I'm goin' to quit this wild west, this bleak and stormy plain,
Where the Indians prowl I'll leave you to ne'er return again

2. I've crossed the Rocky Mountains, I've crossed the rocky hills,
I've crossed the Rocky Mountains where many a brave boy fell.
I've seen the distant country, the Indian and the wild,
I'll never forget that old, old home, and mother's sweetest smile.

3. There was an old rich merchant who lived a neighbor by,
He had the only daughter, on her I cast my eye.
She was most tall and handsome - blue eyes, and curly hair,-
There ain't no one in this wide world to her I can compare.

4. This lady fair and handsome sat closely by my side;
She promised me so faithfully that she would be my bride.
I kissed away those flowing tears still dimming her blue eyes;
I'll never forget that darling girl, I'll love her till I die.

THE NORTHERN COWBOY

111

Sam Bass

*Sam Bass, his fame was such that some unknown minstrels composed a folk ballad about him. . .even said he was a cowboy

Lively

Traditional Cowboy

Sam Bass was born in In-di-an-a, ———— it was his na-tive home, And at the age of sev-en-teen ———— Sam be-gan to roam. When Sam first came out to Tex-as a cow-boy for to be ———— A kind-er heart-ed fel-low ———— you sel-dom ev-er see. ————

*Sam Bass, began his career by robbing stage coaches in the Black Hills. Scenting bigger game in the iron horse, he and a gang of five men in 1877 robbed the express car of a Union Pacific train at Big Springs, Nebraska. Paying him $60,000. and then robbed train after train. He needed money as he was a man of expensive tastes in racehorses, booze and fancy women. Two facts about Bass appealed to the popular imagination. First, he was a generous fellow, paying as much as half a dollar for a chew of tobacco and a $20 gold piece for a panful of hot biscuits (with someone else money of course). Second, he was said to have a habit of burying his loot in unlikely places. Armed with maps or bits of folklore, people searching for the loot were still digging up odd cellars and chopping down hollow trees 50 years after his death. Nobody ever found Sam's money, if it ever existed. But Sam was more notorious than successful as an outlaw, he was mortally wounded in a gunfight with Texas Rangers during a bungled bank robbery in Round Rock, Texas, on July 21, 1878. His dying words were: "Let me go. The world is bobbing around." He was 27 years old

Verse 2
Sam used to deal in race stock, one called the Denton mare;
He matched her in scrub races and took her to the fair.
He used to coin the money, and spent it just as free;
He always drank good whiskey wherever he might be.

Verse 3
Sam he left the Collins ranch, in the early month of May,
With a herd of Texas cattle the Black Hills for to see;
Sold out in Custer City, and then went on a spree-
A tougher set of cowboys you seldom ever see.

Verse 4
On their way back to Texas they robbed the U.P. train,
And then they split up in couples and started out again;
Joe Collins and his partner was overtaken soon,
With all their hard-earned money they had to meet their doom.

Verse 5
Sam had made it back to Texas, all right up with care,
Rode into the town of Denton with all his friends to share.
Sam's life was short in Texas, three robberies did he do;
He robbed all the passenger mail and express cars too.

Verse 6
Sam had four companions, four bold and daring lads,
They were Richardson, Jackson, Joe Collins and Old Dad;
Such bold and daring cowboys the Rangers never knew,
They whipped the Texas Rangers and ran the boys in blue.

Verse 7
Sam and another companion, called "Arkansas" for short,
Was shot by a Texas Ranger by the name of Thomas Floyd;
Oh, Tom is a big six-shooter and thinks he's mighty fly,
But I can tell your his racket-he's a deadbeat on the sly.

Verse 8
Jim Murphy was arrested and then released on bail;
He jumped his bond at Tyler and they took the train for Terrell;
But Mayor Jones had posted Jim and that was all a stall,
It was only a plan to capture sam before the coming fall.

Verse 9
Sam bet his fate at Round Rock, July the twenty-first,
They pierced poor Sam with rifle balls and emptied out his purse.
Sam hi is a corpse and six foot under clay,
An Jackson on the border trying to get away.*

Verse 10
Jim he stole Sam's good gold and he didn't want to pay,
The only shot he saw was to give poor Sam away.
He sold out Sam and Barnes and left their friends to mourn-
Oh, what a scorching Jim should get when Gabriel blows his horn.†

Verse 11
And so he sold out Sam and Barnes and left their friends to mourn-
Oh what a scorching Jim should get when Gabriel blows his horn.
Perhaps he's gone to heaven, there's none of us can say,
But if I am right in my surmise, he's gone the other way.

*Jackson has not been seen, hide nor hair, since that day.
†"I can call to memory Jim Murphy. He was near my age, for we was once schoolboys together. This Jim Murphy gave Sam and his outfit away, and I was told by a man present in the neighborhood where Jim Murphy died that Jim contracted sore eyes because some of Sam's friends slipped deadly poison in Jim's eye medicine and caused him to die a raving maniac."-J.M. Thorne, Fort Worth, Texas.

Cowboy Tidbits

dead man's hand
The poker hand said to have been held by Wild Bill Hickok when he failed to stick to his habit of sitting with his back to the wall and was killed by Jack McCall. Whether this term came from the incident of not, I wouldn't like to swear. The hand? Every Western buff knows it: aces and eights.

devil's lane
Referring to **barb wire.** Many a man has been killed over a fence line . . .. Some land owners dropped back from the survey line and each built his own fence and maintained it, leaving a 10 or 15 foot lane between them. These lanes were referred to as "devils lanes".

dew wrangler
The man who herded horses in the morning.

drag
The rear part of a driven herd of cattle, usually watched over by junior cowhands. An unenviable position, because there a rider swallowed dust and had to contend with animals that could not keep up - sick animals and calves. A day in that position and a man was ready for his blankets at night. To ride drag was sometimes a punishment for bad behavior on the part of the drover. A drag was also a single animal that lagged behind.

draw
(1) Gully; the offshoot of a canyon.
(2) The act of pulling a pistol from a holster.
(3) To **draw a bead.** To take aim with a rifle, by raising the front sight called a bead, to a level with the hind sight.

drift
(1) Used to describe the act of cattle moving ahead of bad weather; or to move almost aimlessly in one direction.
(2) As an extension of this meaning, when a cowboy moved a body of cows easily and without unduly disturbing them, he was said to drift them.
(3) Further extended, the term referred to the movement of a man, meaning simply "to go" -for example, I reckon I'll drift up Cheyenne way.

drovers
The Kansas cattle-town folk and Eastern writers referred to the Texas cattle-trail by this name.

ear-mark
A cut in a cow's ear made in addition to a brand and used to identify an animal when a brand was hidden or obscured. It made a thief's rebranding of a cow more difficult. There were numerous cuts, all of which had individual names, such as *over-slope, under-bit, over-halfcrop, swallow fork,* etc.

-continued on page 125-

Stampede

"For a trailing herd when it's rightly stirred is a thing for a man to shun." No cowboy in his right mind likes a stampede, but Texas Red is the hero here saving the charming miss that blew old Red a kiss. This wonderful poem was first published long ago in the *Wild West Weekly*, New York. Put to music by the talented Derek Cornett, give this song a try.

Music by:
Derek Cornett

© 1994 Centerstream Publishing
All Rights Reserved

1. When the hot sun smiles on the endless miles
That lead to the distant mart,
And the cattle wail down the well-worn trail,
And moan till it grips the heart,
And they gasp for air in the dust clouds there,
As they jostle their way along
With uplifted ear so they may hear
The cow-puncher's evening song.

2. Far up at the head rode old "Texas Red"-
A man of determined face-
And his keen gray eye took in earth and sky
As he rode with a centaur's grace.
On the left was Joe on his white pinto;
Jim Smith patrolled on the right.
And the other tricks took an even six,
And we needed them all that night.

3. And to quench our thirst we had dared the worst
And fought for a nester's well;
But he had a girl with a witching curl,
And she cast a golden spell.
So our shots went wide from the sinner's hide
As he faded from our view,
And the charming miss blew old Red a kiss
And smiled as his pony flew.

4. 'Twas a pretty play, but he spurred away,
His face like a prairie blaze.
And he hit the dirt as he plied his quirt
Till lost in the friendly haze,
While the bawling shrilled as the cattle milled,
And their eyes grew shot with fear-
For they knew right well that a merry hell
Lurked in the gathering smear.

5. In the north black clouds like funeral shrouds
Rolled down with an icy breath,
And we faced a fight on a brutal night
With odds on the side of death;
For a trailing herd when it's rightly stirred
Is a thing for a man to shun,
And no coward band ever holds command
When the norther's on the run.

6. In the ghostly hush that precedes the rush
Of the wild wind-driven flood,
We made our dash to the thunder's crash,
Spurs set till they drew the blood;
But the Storm King struck to our bitter luck,
We rode in the lightning's glare,
And the north wind whirled through a watery world,
And laughed at our puny dare.

7. Then the cattle swerved as a mob unnerved
And shrank from a raging thing,
And they drifted back on the beaten track,
Tail to the norther's sting.
We fought like men, but 'twas useless then-
They plunged down the backward track.
Theirs a single creed - 'twas the dread stampede-
Straight at the nester's shack!

8. There was death at stake, and 'twas made or break
In the rush of that frenzied mob;
But we'd wished our lives in a hundred drives,
And we figured to know our job.
Then a sudden hail on the whistling gale
And a horse went slithering by-
"Twas old Texas Red, and we knew he sped
To the girl of the flashing eye.

9. With a wicked grip on his biting whip,
He smoked down on the heaving ranks,
And his searching eye set to do or die
As he fanned at his pony's flanks;
And we gazed aghast when we saw at last-
Old Tex as the head of the ruck,
And we made a prayer for the rider there,
Just a wish for a hero's luck.

10. Straight she stood and still, at the storm's wild will,
Close by the nester's well,
And her eyes were kissed by the driving mist
As she faced that living hell,
But when Texas Red, 'crost his pony's head,
Erect in his stirrups rose,
Like a sprite she sprung - to his shoulder clung -
A rod from the leader's nose.

11. 'Twas a gallant race, but he held his pace
As he edged to the leeward side.
Not a moment's slip of his strong arm's grip,
As he led that bawling tide;
And his noble steed, knowing well the need,
Gave of his stout heart's best,
And he brought them free from that maddened spree,
And slid - in the mud - to rest.

12. Yes, we found the two where the north wind blew,
Her black hair across his breast;
In his arms she clung as his big heart sung
Under his calfskin vest.
And the lucky brute made us each salute,
And she kissed us one by one,
And we all went wild till old Tex got riled
And threatened to pull a gun.

13. On the trail we lay at the break of day,
Deep in the Texas mud -
Dog-tired we dragged as the cattle lagged,
Cooling their racing blood;
"Twas a weary trek to the river's neck,
And we longed for the scorching sun,
And we drank Red's luck as we downed our chuck,
And we sang - for the night was done!

Stick Close to Your Bedding Ground

By: George Frankson

When the night is black and the storm clouds crack, driv-ing cat-tle wild with fear— There's a light-ning flash and thund-er crash Then a mad stamp-ede is near it's the cow-boy's job to— hold the mob When the herd starts mill-in' 'round— Then in voi-ces strong you will hear this song As the herd is bed-ding down.

Chorus

Now— hush your bawl-in' lit-tle dog-gie— be qui-et now and set-tle down— And you fool-ish old steers, ain't no sense to your fears, Stick— close to your bed-din' ground— The— flash-in' light-nin' is the lan-tern— of the big boss in the sky— And the thund-er's the noise of the boss and his boys Rid-in'

When the night is black and the storm clouds crack,
    driving cattle wild with fear
There's a lightning flash and thunder crash,
    then a mad stampede is near
It's the cowboys job to hold that mob,
    when the herd starts millin' 'round
Then in voices strong you will hear this
    song as the herd is bedded down.
Chorus:
Now hush your bawlin' little doggie be
    quiet now and settle down
And you foolish old steers, ain't no sense to your fears,
    stick close to your beddin' ground
The flashin' lightin' in the lantern of the
    big boss in the sky
And the thunder's the noise of the boss and
    his boys, ridin' herd at the ranch on high
So wait for the sun little doggie,
    for the sun and a bright new day,
Wait for the sun little doggie,
    to chase the storm away
Now hush your bawlin' little doggie be
    quiet now and settle down,
And you foolish old steers ain't no sense to your fears,
    stick close to your bedding ground.

Now a cowboy ain't a plaster saint,
    with golden harp and wings
While angel songs and op'ra songs,
    ain't the kind the cowboy sings
Yet his cheerful words will quiet herds,
    and calm and safety bring
Will meet the need when herds stampede,
    so listen while he sings.
Chorus:
Now hush your bawlin' little doggie old
    mammy cow quit moanin' 'round
And you foolish old steers, ain't no sense to your fears,
    stick close to your beddin' ground
The flashin' lightin' in the lantern of the
    big boss in the sky
And the thunder's the noise of the boss and his boys,
    ridin' herd at the ranch on high
So wait for the sun little doggie,
    for the sun and a bright new day,
Wait for the sun little doggie,
    to chase the storm away
Now hush your bawlin' little doggie
    ol mammy cow quit moanin' 'round
And you foolish old steers ain't no sense to your fears,
    stick close to your bedding ground.

Ten Thousand Cattle

Owen Wister who wrote <u>The Virginian</u> composed this song in 1888.

Old Cowboy Song

Ten thousand cattle, gone astray,
Left my range and traveled away,
And the sons-of-guns, I'm here to say,
Have left me dead broke, dead broke today.

Refrain:
In gambling hells delaying,
Ten thousand cattle straying, ten thousand cattle straying.

And my gal, she has gone away,
Left my shacd and traveled away,
With a son-of-a gun from Ioway,
And left me a lone man, a lone man today.

Refrain:
In gambling hells delaying,
Ten thousand cattle straying, ten thousand cattle straying.

She was awful sweet and loved me so
But the Ioway fellow made her go.
Now my heart is broke, and I'm weak and low,
And to drink my life away is all I know.

Refrain:
In gambling hells delaying,
Ten thousand cattle straying, ten thousand cattle straying.

I had a ranch and cattle on the plains
And every year my business showed a gain
But when she left me, it caused me ache and pain
And I'll never try to build a home again.

Refrain:
In gambling hells delaying,
Ten thousand cattle straying, ten thousand cattle straying.

THREE THOUSAND TEXAS STEERS

Words by Ben Thorne
(to the tune of "The Wandering Cowboy")

"Way down in lower Texas
Along the Southern line,
We bunched 3,000 longhorns
In the spring of '79;
Three thousand wild old coast steers
Road branded "Lazy L".
All the way up that trail, boys.
We shorely did smell hell.

Spike Jenkins was our ramrod;
A grand old scout was he.
We crossed the River Concho,
The boy he saved was me.
Two of us in the whirlpool,
And one must there go down
Never to reach his destination,
The Ogallala town.

But now those rollicky beef steers
Forced our attention and time
And they took us on a dirty race
Before we crossed the line.
It was three nights out from the Brazos,
They made a nasty run;
Every puncher in the saddle
From dusk till morning's sun.

"How many are there missing?"
We took them through the count.
When we got our final tally,
We were ninety big steers out.
So we rode that country over
For many miles around,
And that night forty beef-steers
Walked in on the bed ground.

"So it's throw them on the trail, boys;
Yonder rolls the mighty Red!
Tonight we sleep in the Indian country,
With these 3,000 head".
Now there is an old-time maxim;
It's "Look before you leap".
It was easier said than done:
Old Red flowed wide and deep.

"I'll bust her on the point," said Spike.
"Boys, you feed 'em in the swing,
And we'll cross the raging torrent
As if we were all on wing."
With the Concho Twin on the east side point,
And old Spike on the left,
We brought 'em down to the entering point,
A hundred steers abreast.

They took the water with a rush,
The current they seemed to ride.
Soon the cattle and the punchers
Were swimming side by side.
Those muddy waters beat 'round us,
Like boat in a stormy sea,
But we all landed safely
In the big I.T.*

*(Indian Territory)

119

The Big Corral

Arizona cowboy and entertainer Romaine Lowdermilk wrote this song in 1922.
The song pokes fun at the camp cook and was based on an English gospel tune.

Lively   *Cowboy Song*

That ug-ly brute from the cat-tle chute, Press a-long to the big cor-ral. He should be brand-ed on the snoot, Press a-long to the big cor-ral. Press a-long cow-boy, Press a-long with a cow-boy yell. Press a-long with a noise, big noise, Press a-long to the big cor-ral.

That ugly brute from the cattle chute,
Press along to the Big Corral.
He should be branded on the snoot,
Press along to the Big Corral.

Chorus:

Press along cowboy,
Press along with a cowboy yell.
Press along with a noise, big noise,
Press along to the Big Corral.

Early in the morning 'bout half-past four,
Press along to the Big Corral.
You'll hear him open his face to roar,
Press along to the Big Corral.

Chorus

The wrangler's out a-combing the hills,
Press along to the Big Corral.
So jump in your britches and grease up your gills,
Press along to the Big Corral.

Chorus

The chuck we get ain't fit to eat,
Press along to the Big Corral.
There's rocks in the beans and sand in the meat,
Press along to the Big Corral.

Chorus

That ugly gink is a half-breed Chink,
Press along to the Big Corral.
He makes our biscuits in the sink,
Press along to the Big Corral.

Chorus

The Bronk That Would'nt Bust

What's a buster to do when he finds a bronk that can't be rode?
Read the last two lines of verse 4.

Cowboy Song

1. I've busted bronchos off an' on since first I hit their trail
An' you bet I savvy bronchos from nostrils down to tail
But I struck one on Powder River, say hands he was the first,
An' only liven bronchos yours truly couldn't bust.

Yodel:
Lay - lay - ee - lee -o - lee - o lay - lay-lee - lee
Lay - lay- ee - lee o - lee- o -lee

2. He was a no account buckskin, wasn't worth two bits to keep
Had a black stripe down his backbone an' was wooly like a sheep
That horse wasn't built to tread the earth, he took natural to the air,
An' ev'ry time he went a loft, he tried to leave me there.
Yodel:

3. He went so high above the earth Light from cross Jorden shone
Right there we parted company an' he came down alone
I hit ole terra firma, The broncho's heels struck free
An' brought a bunch of stars along to dance in front of me.
Yodel:

4. I'm not a riden airships nor electric flyin' beasts
I ain't got rich relations awaiting me back east
So I've sold my chaps and saddle, my spurs can lay and rust,
For there's now and then a broncho that a buster can not bust.
Yodel:

121

The California Stage Company

This old poem put to new music by Derek Cornett tells about traveling on the California stage line, starting off with "There's no respect for youth or age" and goes down hill from there.

Music by :
Derek Cornett

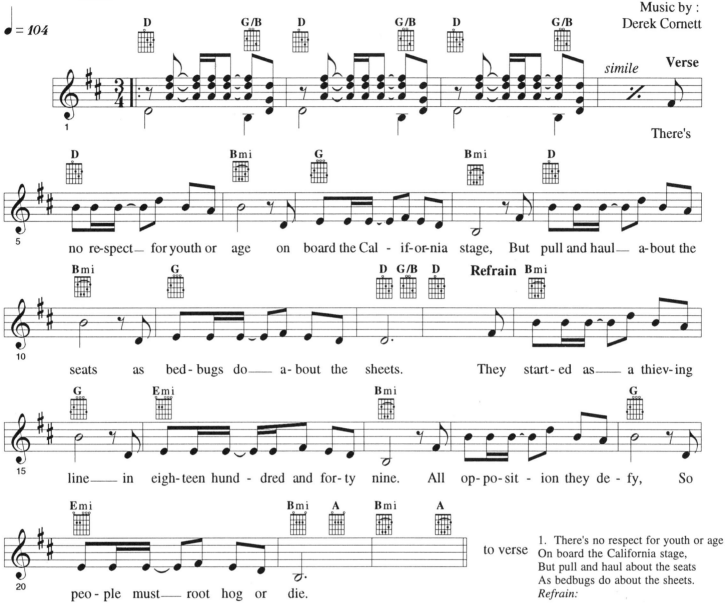

1. There's no respect for youth or age
   On board the California stage,
   But pull and haul about the seats
   As bedbugs do about the sheets.
   Refrain:

2. They started as a thieving line
   In eighteen hundred and forty-nine;
   All opposition they defy,
   So the people must root hog or die.
   Refrain:

3. You're crowded in with Chinamen,
   As gattening hogs are in a pen;
   And what will more a man provoke
   Is musty plug tobacco smoke.
   Refrain:

4. The ladies are compelled to sit
   With dresses in tobacco spit;
   The gentlemen don't seem to care,
   But talk on politics and swear.
   Refrain:

5. The dust is deep in summer time,
   The mountains very hard to climb,
   And drivers often stop and yell,
   "Get out, all hands, and push uphill."
   Refrain:

6. The drivers, when they feel inclined,
   Will have you walking on behind,
   And on your shoulders lug a pole
   To help them out some muddy hole.
   Refrain:

7. They promise when your fare you pay,
   "You'll have to walk but half the way";
   Then add aside, with cunning laugh,
   "You'll have to push the other half."
   Refrain:

8. They have and will monopolize
   The business till the people rise,
   And send them kiting down below
   To start to live with Bates and Rowe.
   Refrain:

© 1994 Centerstream Publishing
All Rights Reserved

The Cowboy

This song was written in 1885 by Allen McCandless. Sometimes this song is called the COWBOY'S SOLILOQUY.

Based upon "Cowboyin'"
by: Frank W. Chamberlin

Moderato

All day on the prai - rie in the sad - dle I ride, Not ev - en a dog, boys, to trot by my side. My fire I must kin - dle with chips gath - ered 'round And boil my own cof - fee with - out be - ing ground. I wash in a pool and I wipe on a sack I— car - ry my ward - robe all on my back.

For want of an oven I cook bread in a pot
And sleep on the ground for want of a cot.
My ceiling's the sky, my floor is the grass;
My music's the lowing of the herds as they pass.
My books are the brooks and my sermons the stones;
My parson's a wolf on his pulpit of bones.

And then if my cooking is not very complete,
You can't blame me for wanting to eat.
But show me a man that sleeps more profound
Than the big puncher-boy who's stretched out on the ground.
My books teach me ever consistence to prize,
My sermons, that small things I should n ot despise.

My parson remarks from his pulpit of bones
That fortune favors those who look out for their own.
And between me and love lies a gulf very wide.
Some lucky fellow may call her his bride.
My friends gently hint I am coming to grief,
But men must make money and women have beef.

But Cupid is always a friend to the bold,
And the best of his arrows are pointed with gold.
Society bans me so savage and dodge
That the Masons would ball me out of their lodge.
If I'd hair on my chin, I might pass for the goat
That bore all the sins in the ages remote.

But why it is I can never understand,
For each of the patriarchs owned a big brand.
Abraham emigrated in search of a'range,
And when water was scarce he wanted a change.
Old Isaac owned cattle in charge of Esau,
And Jacob punched cows for his father-in-law.

He started in business way down at bed rock,
And made quite a streak at handling stock.
David went from night-herding to using a sling;
And, winning the battle, he became a great king.
Then the shepherds, while herding the sheep on a hill,
Got a message from heaven of peace and goodwill.

A TEXAS COWPUNCHER

The Cowboy's Dream

Written in 1873 by Charley Hart, original title was "Drift to That Sweet By-and-By." This song was a favorite of the Texas evangelist, Rev. Abe Mulkey, when urging the cowboys to "come up to the mourners' bench" at the frontier camp meetings. The tune is *My Bonnie Lies Over the Ocean.* A religious allegory' the head man makes room for strays and "they say he will never forget you." "Get branded," is the advice, and "have your name in his big tally book."

Words and Music by
Charley Hart

Pensively

Last night as I lay on the prai - rie,_____ And looked at the stars in the sky,_____ I won - dered if ev - er a cow - boy_____ Would drift to that sweet by - and - by.

Refrain

Roll on, Roll on; Roll on, lit - tle do - gies, roll on. Roll on, roll on, roll on; Roll on, lit - tle do - gies, roll on._____

fine

124

Last night as I lay on the prairie,
And looked at the stars in the sky,
I wondered if ever a cowboy
Would drift to that sweet by-and-by.

Refrain:
Roll on, roll on;
Roll on, little dogies, roll on.
Roll on, roll on, roll on;
Roll on, little dogies, roll on.

The road to that bright happy region
Is a dim narrow trail, so they say;
But the bright one that leads to perdition
Is posted and blazed all the way.

Oh, bring back, bring back,
Bring back my night horse to me.
Oh, bring back, bring back,
Bring back my night horse to me.

They say there will be a great round-up.
And cowboys, like dogies, will stand,
To be mavericked by the Riders of Judgment
Who are posted and know every brand.

I know there's many a stray cowboy
Who'll be lost at the great final sale,
When he might have gone in green pastures
Had he known the dim narrow trail.

I wonder if ever a cowboy
Stood ready for that Judgment Day
And could say to the Boss of the Riders,
"I'm ready, come drive me away."

For they, like the cows that are locoed,
Stampede at the sight of a hand,
Are dragged with a rope to the round-up,
Or get marked with some crooked man's brand.

And I'm scared that I'll be a stray yearling
A maverick, unbranded on high -
And cut* in the bunch with the "rusties"†
When the Boss of the Riders goes by.

I often look upward and wonder
If the green fields will seem half so fair,
If any the wrong trail have taken
And will fail to be over there.

No maverick or slick‡ will be tallied
In that great book of life in his home,
For he knows all the brands and the earmarks
That down through the ages have come.

But along with the strays and the sleepers,
The tailings must turn from the gate;
No road brand to give them admission,
But that awful sad cry, "Too late!"

For they tell of another big owner
Who's ne'er overstocked, so they say,
But who always makes room for the sinner
Who drifts from the strait narrow way.

They say he will never forget you,
That he knows every action and look;
So, for safety, you'd better get branded,
Have your name in his big Tally Book,

To be shipped to that bright mystic region,
Over there in the green pastures to lie,
And be led by the crystal still waters
To the home in the sweet by-and-by.

* Cutting cattle not suitable for driving up the trail
† Underdeveloped cattle
‡ "Maverick" and "slicks" are unbranded cattle. "Slicks"
   are young cattle lightly branded by thieves who plan
   to come back later and steal them

> Singing to a herd of thousands of cattle to sleep was not an unusual undertaking in the days when the old Chisholm Trail was the great driveway between Texas ranches and the railroad shipping points in Kansas. Round and round the herd the riders would go. "Say, my voice is getting mighty tired," one of the riders would call out. "Can't one of you fellers tune up and give me a rest?" An other rider would take up the song, and the cattle would slumber the night through. One of the favorites is *The Dim Narrow Trail,* or *The Cowboy's Dream.*"
> —*San Antonio Express* (May 30, 1909)

Cowboy Tidbits

exalted
To be uplifted by a rope drawn tightly around the neck - in short: hanged. A nice touch of macabre Western humor.
fandango
(Sp; SW) A lively dance, with castanets and in triple measure. Also used to describe a party or celebration.
faro
In the eighteenth century, the work was *faroon* (said to be from the French work *pharaon,* meaning pharaoh, which stood for the king of hearts in a pack of playing cards). A game, popular in the gambling halls of the West, in which the players bet on the order that cards would be drawn from a box. Traditionally there was a tiger painted on this box, hence the expressions to *buck* or *fight the tiger.* Not a Westernism.
fill a blanket
To roll a cigarette.
flank riders
Trail riders who guard a trail-herd behind the swing riders, who were behind the point riders; at the rear came the drag.
flannel mouth
An overly talkative man, a boaster.
flea-bag
Sleeping bag.
flea-trap
A bed-roll.
following the tongue
In order to set his course for the following day, a trail-boss might point the tongue of his wagon at the polestar during the night.
fool brand
One so complicated in its design or so difficult to read that it defied description.
fumadiddle
Fancy dress.

-continued on page 127-

The Cowboy's Prayer

Written in 1907 by Charles Badger Clark Jr. One of the first and very best Cowboy Poets, when he was living in Southeastern Arizona. His work is among the most recited, most sung and probably the most recorded of any Western poet. This is one of his best songs. Here the cowboy asks God to bless the cattle range. The round-up has been blessed through the years, but "don't forget the growing steers." The cowboy's concern for his animals is shown in his request for rain, for the cessation of prairie fires. "Our mountains are peaceful, Our prairies serene. O Lord, for the cattle, Please keep them clean."

(Instrumental Intro)

Oh Lord please hear——me lend me thine ear. The prayer of a trou-bled cow-boy to hear. No doubt the prayer may seem to be strange,—— but I ask you to bless our cat - tle range. *(Inst. between verses)*

Verse 2
You bless the round-up through the year,
Now please don't forget the steer;
Water the land with brooks and rills
For the cattle that roam on a thousand hills.

Verse 3
The prarie fires, won't you please stop?
Make thunder roll, make the rain to drop.
Our mountains are peaceful, our prarie serene.
Oh Lord for the cattle, please keep them green.

126

The Cowboy's Stroll

Smoothly

Tune: "The Nightingale"

One eve-ning, one eve-ning, one eve-ning, in May, I spied a fair maid-en a-rak-ing of hay. "Good eve-ning, I'm glad of meet-ing you here, Al-tho' you're a la-dy and I'm a ran-ger."

1. One evening, one evening, one evening in May,
I spied a fair maiden a raking of hay.
"Good evening, I'm glad of meeting you here,
Altho' you're a lady and I'm a ranger."

2. They walked and they talked till they came to a spring,
And from his knap sack he drew a fine violin.
"Good evening I'm glad of meeting you here,
Altho' you're a lady and I'm a ranger."

3. And now says the lady, "Just play one tune more,"
And now says the lady, "Just play an encore."
He tuned up his fiddle to a much higher string,
And he played her a tune called "The Valleys Do Ring."

4. And then says the lady, "Won't you marry me?"
"Oh", says the cowboy, "that never can be:
I've a wife in old Texas and children three,
And the prettiest wee baby you ever did see."

5. "I'll go back to Texas and stay there one year;
I will drink of cold water instead of strong beer.
And if I return it well be in the spring,
To see the water gliding and hear the nightingale sing.

6. "I will build me a castle in some Texas town,
So strong that no wind can blow it down,
And if anyone asks if I live alone,
Pray, tell them I'm a cowboy far away from home."

Cowboy Tidbits

girls of the line
Prostitutes. So called because the women plied their trade in shacks and tents drawn up in lines on the outskirts of cowtowns, mining camps, and railroad end-of-track camps.

greasy sack outfit
A poor cattle-outfit so needy that they were forced to carry their supplies in greasy sacks. In the earliest cattle drives from Texas, as in the cowhunts of that period, each of the few men involved carried his own food. He might take it in a saddlebag or in a sack tied behind the cantle of his saddle . . . In the later years, one that persisted in this method was called a 'greasy sack' outfit.

G.T.T.
In the Southeast, when a man wanted by the law could not be located, lawmen entered in their records "G.T.T." - Gone to Texas. Which was most likely correct, for Texas as a good place in which to make a new start with the slate wiped clean. The initials were also used by folks who upped stakes for a new start in the Lone Star State and left the information G.T.T. marked on their doors.

hoolihan
(1) The act of throwing a grown steer by hand, but without using the twisting movement of **bulldogging**. Usually a rider would jump from the back of a running horse across the back of a running cow, landing behind its horns in such a way as to knock it down without using the usual wrestling hold - a practice not regarded favorably and disallowed in most rodeos.
This term was sometimes mistakenly corrupted to hooley-ann.
(2) To behave roughly, to celebrate wildly in town.
(3) When a horse, in fighting its rider, somersaults.

Indian shod
A method of horse-shoeing employed at times by most Indian peoples. The usual procedure was to cover the whole foot with damp rawhide, which, when dried, fitted the foot snugly and became very hard. Most of the mustang stock of the Indians was hard-footed, but the best horse with unshod hoofs would suffer after working too long in rocky country.

-continued on page 133-

The Cowboy's Warning

Words and Music by:
Babe Buzan
Harry Walters
& Nellie Garwood Vaughn

The Crooked Trail to Holbrook

In 1882 the railroad reached Holbrook in Arizona Territory. This became the major shipping point for cattle from all over East Central Arizona. This song, obviously written by someone who knew the trail well, tells of a cattle drive from the Globe area to the pens in Holbrook. The Trail wound through some of the roughest country in all of Arizona. The Holbrook Trail was still in use as late as 1943

Come all you jol - ly cow - boys who fol - low the bron - co steer. I'll sing for you a verse or two, your spir - its for to cheer. I'll tell you 'bout a lit - tle trip that I did un - der - go, on the crook - ed trail to Hol - brook, in Ar - i - zon - i - o.

Come all you jolly cowboys who follow the bronco steer,
I'll sing to you a verse or two, your spirits for to cheer.
I'll tell you all about a trip that I did undergo
On the crooked trai lto Holbrook, in Arizon-i-o.

On February the seventeenth our herd it started out.
It would have made you shudder to hear them bawl and shout.
As wild as any buffalo that ever roamed the Platte,
The cattle we were driving, and every one was fat.

We crossed the Mescal Mountains and how the wind did blow.
A blizzard was a-raging and the pass was deep in snow.
But the pointers kept 'em headed and the drag men pushed 'em slow
On the crooked trail to Holbrook, in Arizon-i-o.

One night we had a stampede- Lord, how the cattle run!
We made it to our horses, but boys it was no fun.
Over prickly pear and catclaw brush we quickly made our way,
We thought of our long journey and the girls we left one day.

When we got to Gilson Flats, the wind did surely blow.
It blew so hard and blew so fierce, we knew not where to go.
But our spirits never failed us as onward we did go
On the crooked trail to Holbrook, in Arizon-i-o.

It's along by Sombrero we slowly punched along,
While each and every puncher would sing a hearty song.
To cheer up all his comrades as onward we did go
On the crooked trail to Holbrook, in Arizon-i-o.

We crossed the rugged Mogollon where tall pine forests grow.
The grass was in abundance and rippling streams did flow.
Our packs were always turning, of course our gait was slow
On the crooked trail to Holbrook, in Arizon-i-o.

At last we got to Holbrook and a little breeze did blow.
It blew up sand and pebbles and it didn't blow them slow.
We had to drink the water from that muddy little stream,
And swallowed a peck of gravel when we tried to eat a bean.

And when the herd was sold and shippped and homeward we were bound
With as tired a string of horses as ever could be found.
Across the reservation, no danger did we fear,
We thought of wives and sweethearts, the ones we loved so dear.

We're now back in Globe City, our friendships there to share.
Here's luck to every puncher who follows the bronco steer.
My best advice to you, boys, is try and never go
On the crooked trail to Holbrook, in Arizon-i-o.

The Dreary Black Hills

Traditional Cowboy

Sadly

Kind folks you will pit-y my hor-ri-ble tale; I'm an ob-ject that's need-y and look-ing quite stale. I gave up my trade, sell-ing Wright's Pat-ent Pills, To go dig-ging for gold in the drear-y Black Hills.

Chorus

Don't go a-way stay at home if you can, Far a-way from that cit-y they call it Chey-enne, For old Sit-ting Bull and Co-man-che Bill Will raise up your hair in the drear-y Black Hills.

In Cheyenne the round House is filled up every night
With Pilgrims of every description in sight:
No clothes on their backs, in their pockets no bills,
And yet they are striding out for the Black Hills.

(Chorus)

When I came to the Black Hills, no gold could I find,
I thought of the Free Lunch I left far behind;
Through rain, hail and sleet, nearly froze to the gills,
They call me the orphan boy of the Black Hills.

(Chorus)

Oh, I wish that the man who first started this sell
Was a captive, and Crazy Horse had him in-well,
There is no use in grieving or swearing like pitch,
But the man who would stay there is a son of a bitch.

(Chorus)

So now to conclude, this advice I'll unfold,
Don't come to the Black Hills a-looking for gold.
For Big Wallapie and Comanche Bill
Are scouting, I'm told, in the dreary Black Hills.

Sitting Bull, Teton Dakota Indian chief.

A party of gold prospectors, maybe former cowboys, who died of starvation in the Dreary Black Hills. Well, maybe it wasn't the Black Hills but the dangers faced by those searching the mountains for gold were real enough-accidents in remote areas, bad weather, hostile Indians, wild animals, little food or water in some locations, impure water and rampant disease in others. It would be impossible to calculate the number of lives lost to the search for gold.

The Dreary, Dreary Life

Published in 1908 by Jack Thorpe, this song seems to have been based on a Lumberjack song.

Old Cowboy Song

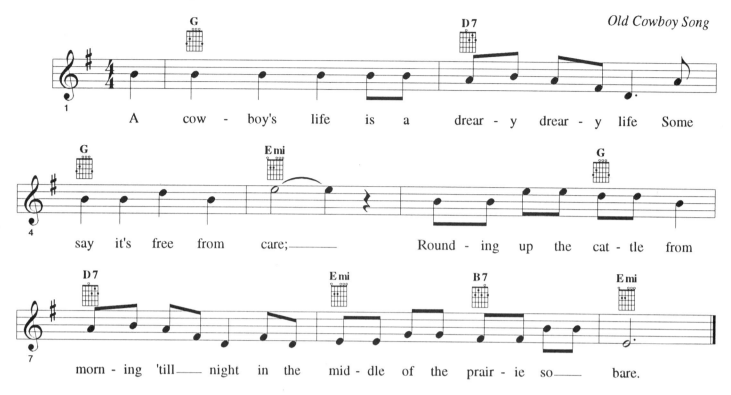

A cow-boy's life is a drear-y drear-y life Some say it's free from care;—— Round-ing up the cat-tle from morn-ing 'till—— night in the mid-dle of the prair-ie so—— bare.

A cowboy's life is a dreary, dreary life
Some say it's free from care;
Rounding up the cattle from morning till night
In the middle of the prairie so bare.

Half-past four the noisy cook will roar,
"Whoop -a whoop-a hey"
Slowly you will rise with sleepy feeling eyes
The sweet dreamy night passed away.

The cowboy's life is a dreary, dreary life,
He's driven through heat and cold;
While the rich man's sleeping on his velvet couch,
Dreaming of his silver and gold.

Spring-time sets in, double trouble will begin,
The weather is fierce and cold;
Clothes are wet and frozen to our necks,
The cattle we can scarcely hold.

The wolves and owls with their terrifying howls
Will disturb our midnight dream,
As we lie on our slickers on a cold, rainy night
"Way over on the Pecos stream.

The cowboys life is a dreary, dreary one
He's riding through the heat and cold
I used to run about now I stay at home
Take care of my wife and child.

**Cigar box label
c. 1890**

A VANISHING AMERICAN ART FORM

DOBRO OF *COURSE*

Little Buckaroos pickin' and grinnin'

Singing "Songs Around The Campfire,"
Ad reprint of the 1928 Dobro Guitar Company,
Courtesy of John Quartman

Cowboy Tidbits

jingle bob
(1) The cattle *ear-mark* of John Chisum of Billy the Kid fame. It was a complete slitting of the ear from the tip to the base, giving the animal a somewhat grotesque appearance, as if it had two ears on either side of its head, one standing up and the other drooping. Chisum cattle were so famous for this ear-mark that they were known as **jingle bobs** and the crew were known as the **jingle bob outfit.** (2) The jingles on a cowboy's spurs.

love apples
Canned tomatoes.

meat biscuit
(1) The concentrated juice of beef, mixed with flour and baked. It is chiefly used to make soup for travelers and soldiers, etc.
(2)Canned beef, first produced in Texas in the early 1850s by Gail Borden, who later made a fortune canning condensed milk.

Mexican strawberries
Beans.

poppers
In the early days, cattlemen were to be found driving cattle with whips having a popper - a separate strip of buckskin - attached at the end of the lash to add a louder not to the cracking of the whip. For this same reason, it was not uncommon through all the trail-driving years to find drovers with buckskin poppers at the end of their ropes.

put on tallow
In reference to cattle, to put on fat. The word *tallow* was used no doubt because in Texas, before a good market was found for live cattle, men who owned Longhorns had to find other ways of turning cows into cash, and one of them was to send them to the tallow factories. Many a Texas candle burned on the tallow of cattle.

range bum
A man riding from ranch to ranch for free meals; a *chuck-line rider.* An out-of-work cowhand. Depressions hit the cattle-trade as they did any other in the last quarter of the nineteenth century.

range delivery
If a man bought cattle range delivery, he bought cattle on a range, accepting the estimate of the seller. This was a gamble taken fairly frequently and sometimes great profit was made - as much as a 1.000 head over the estimate. The term is indicative of the times - the word of a man of good reputation was trusted.

roll his tail
(1) A cow that intends to run will hump up its tail at the body end, a telltale sign. **Rolling their tails** describes stampeding cattle. Hence: (2) The act of a man departing on the run.

rodeo
Originally used solely to refer to the annual round-up of cattle, burrowed directly into American-English from the Mexicans and Californios in the first half of the 19th century. Only toward the end of the century did it take on its present meaning.

soiled dove
A prostitute. A Victorianism beloved of newspapermen and contemporary literature. Not truly a Westernism, but found fairly frequently in Western writings.

sowbosom
Salt pork, **sowbelly,**. One of a number of Western euphemisms to be used in the presence of ladies.

133

-continued on page 138-

The Dying Outlaw

The last words and wishes of a cowboy waiting to ride in that great rodeo in the sky

♩ = 116

Edith Fowke

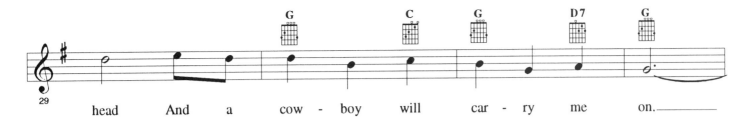

head   And   a   cow - boy   will   car - ry   me   on.____

1.   last time

____   eo.____

I've rode on the prairie by night and by day,
No danger I feared as I rode along;
But a red-coated foreman has written my doom,
And a cowboy will carry me on.

Be kind to my pony while with you he stays,
Then bury him beside me when he must go,
How often I've tried him and I know he won't fail
When we ride in that great rodeo.

THE ELEVEN SLASH SLASH ELEVEN
tune: "The Chisholm Trail"

It's round up your cavy and it's rope out your pack,
And strap your old kack well fast on his back;

Refrain:
Singing hi yi yippy, yippy, hi, yippy yea,
Singing hi yi yippy, yippy yea.

Your foot in your stirrup and your hand on the horn,
You're the best damn cowboy that ever was born;

You land in the saddle and give a loud yell,
For the longhorn cattle have got to take the hill;

You round up a bunch of dogies and take down the trail,
But the first thing, you land in jail;

But the sheriff's an old puncher and he fixes your bail,
It's a damn poor country with a cowboy in jail;

So you round in your foreman and you hit him for your roll,
For you're going to town to act a little bold;

You strap on your chaps, your spurs and your gun,
For you're going to town and have a little fun;

And ride a big bronc that will buck and prance,
And you pull out your gun and make the tenderfoot dance;

You go into the gambling house a-looking kinder funny,
For you got every pocket just chock full of money;

You play cards with a gambler who's got a marked pack,
And you walk back to the ranch with the saddle on your back;

Now, I've punched cattle from Texas to Maine,
And I've known some cowboys by their right name;

No matter, though, whatever they claim,
You'll find every dirty cuss exactly the same;

So dig in your spurs and peel your eyes to heaven,
But never overlook a calf with Eleven Slash Slash Eleven;

Wayne Horsburgh

135

The Face In My Campfire

Words and Music by:
Sheriff Tucker, Elsa Barton
and Gladys Helle

My pon-y and me are leg wea-ry———— Our night - herd - ing

days are through———— We've gone to the ends of the rain - bow,————

——— But the trail leads back to you.———————— It's

Refrain: your face I see in my camp-fire to - night, It out-shines the stars and the

moon's sil - vr'y light, I left you in tears and have roamed all these years But each

night in my camp-fire your dear face ap - pears; No long - er I'll search for

hid - den gold in the moun - tains and streams.————————

I on-ly search for that heart of gold I see ev'-ry night in my

dreams. _____ It's your face I see in my camp-fire to - night, 'Twill be

ling - er - ing on 'til the dawns ear - ly light, I feel your em - brace as the

1.

trail I re - trace to the face in my camp-fire to - night. It's

2.

night. _____

Patsy Montana

137

The Ghost of Jim Lane

A ghostly tale of drinkin', riddin', and the night Jim Lane went to jail

Slow Waltz Time   *Old Cowboy Song*

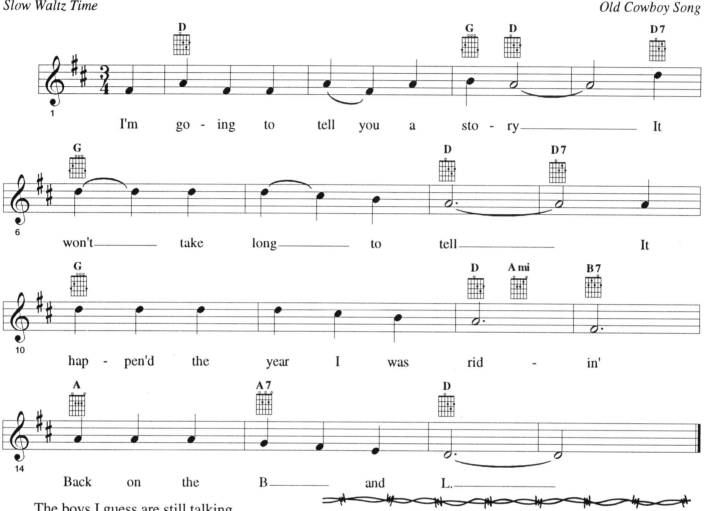

I'm go-ing to tell you a sto-ry_____ It
won't____ take long____ to tell____ It
hap-pen'd the year I was rid - in'
Back on the B____ and L.____

The boys I guess are still talking
About that fatal night.
The Ghost of Jim Lane got a walkin'
Shot out the barroom light.

We're sittin' a-round kind of mournful,
Seems Jim had rode away.
And no one a-knowed where he'd went to,
Or just how long he would stay.

The Sheriff had rode away with him;
They took the bottom trail.
And Jim he was swearin' to Heaven
They couldn't keep him in jail.

We're sittin' and drinkin', when sudden
The door swung open wide,
And somethin' that looked like hereafter
Came slippin' down inside.

A shot, and the light went out crashin',
The way they tell the tale.
That just was the time Jim was shot through
Tryin' to break the jail.

Cowboy Tidbits

spilling   stock
Allowing stock to scatter while driving them.

spurs
The spur is composed of a heel-band, a shank, and, commonly, a rowel. Roughly speaking, the fashion in spurs showed some difference east and west of the Rockies, as in so many other things concerning horses and horsemen. The California spur, true to the Spanish-Mexican influence, tended to be more highly decorated and larger. Shanks could be straight or curved, the curves described according to their depth: one-third, a quarter, half, or full curve. The Old Californios favored so great a curve that the spur had to be removed on dismounting if the owner wished to walk. The Mexican style fitted to the boot-heel, the Anglo to the foot-heel. The Californians wore their spurs loose with a chain under the instep of the foot, while most Anglos wore a tight strap. Rowels were of various design but usually took the shape of wheels and stars.

Most spurs look much alike to the uninitiated, but to the horseman there is a great difference between them. In fact, bring two horsemen together and raise the subject and you'll get as good an argument as you would if you started comparing the dally system of roping with the hard-and-fast style. To the modern city man, the spur seems a cruel and barbarous piece of equipment, but, as with a bit, a spur is as cruel as the man using it. A large, savage-looking Mexican spur used to be no more painful to a horse than a small one; indeed, the small spur with a single spike is more likely to be cruel. The horseman of the Old West, particularly the Californian, used the spur for guidance and as an emergency starter. In fact, the judicious use of his armed heels saved many a vaquero from coming off worst in a disagreement with a ladino on the prod.

-continued on page 155-

The Girl I Left Behind Me

More than likely of Irish ancestry, this song dates back to at least the 1700s.

Cowboy Song

I struck the trail in sev-en-ty nine, The herd strung out be-hind me. As I jogged a-long my mind went back to the girl I left be-hind me. That sweet lit-tle girl, that true lit-tle girl, the girl I left be-hind me. That sweet lit-tle girl, that true lit-tle girl, the girl I left be-hind me.

I struck the trail in '79,
The herd strung out behind me.
As I jogged along my mind went back
To the girl I left behind me.

Chorus:
That sweet little girl, that true little girl,
The girl I left behind me;
That sweet little girl, that true little girl,
The girl I left behind me.

If ever I get off the trail,
And the Indians they don't find me,
I'll go right back where I belong
To the girl I left behind me.

Chorus

The night was dark and the cattle run,
With the boys coming on behind me.
My mind went back at my pistol's crack
To the girl I left behind me.

Chorus

The wind did blow; the rain did flow;
The hail did fall and blind me.
And I thought of her, that sweet little girl,
The girl I left behind me.

Chorus

She wrote ahead to the place I said,
And I was glad to find it.
She said, "I'm true, when you get through,
Ride back and you will find me."

Chorus

When we sold out, I took the train;
I knew where I could find her.
When I got back we had a smack,
And I'm no gol-durned liar.

Chorus

The Hills Of Mexico

This is a version of the old BUFFALO SKINNERS song. It is about the Goodnight-Loving Trail.

Old Cowboy Song

It was in the town of Griffin
In the year of '83,
When an old cowpuncher stepped up
And this he said to me:
"Howdy do, young feller
And how'd you like to go
And spend a pleasant summer
Out in New Mexico?"

I, being out of employment,
To the puncher I did say:
"Depends upon the wages
That you will have to pay.
You pay to me good wages
And transportation too,
And I think that I will go with you
One summer season through."

We left the town of Griffin
In the merry month of May.
the flowers were all blooming
And everything seemed gay.
Our trip it was a pleasure
The road we had to go
Until we reached Old Boggy
Out in New Mexico.

It was there our pleasures ended
And troubles then begun.
The first hailstorm came on us,
Oh, how those cattle run!
Through mesquite, thorns, and thickets
We cowboys had to go,
While the Indians watched our pickets
Out in New Mexico.

And when the drive was over,
The foreman wouldn't pay.
To all of you good people
This much I have to say:
"With guns and rifles in our hands
I'll have you all to know,
We left his bones to bleach upon
The Hills of Mexico."

And now the drive is over
And homeward we are bound.
No more in this damned old country
Will ever I be found.
Back to friends and loved ones
And tell them not to go
To the God-forsaken country
They call New Mexico.

The Jolly Cowboy Song

Rather Slowly

The Roaming Ranger
and Joe Davis

me my quirt___ and pon - y,___ I'm read - y for this

trail;___I love the roll - ing prair - ies,___ They're

free from care___ and strife,___ Be - hind a herd___ of

Long - horns,___I'll journ - ey all my life.___

D.C. back to verse

1. My lover he is a Cowboy, he's brave and kind and true;
He rides a Spanish pony, he throws a lasso, too;
And when he comes to see me, our vows we do redeem
He throws his arms around me, and thus begins to sing.

2. When early dawn is breaking, and we are far away;
We fall into our saddles, we round up all the day;
We rope, we brand we earmark, I tell you we are smart,
And when the herd is ready, for Kansas then we start.

3. When threat'ning clouds do gather, and herded lightnings flash,
And heavy rain drops splatter, and rolling thunders crash;
What keeps the herd from running, stampeding far and wide?
The Cowboys long, low whistle, and singing by their side.

142

The Lone Star Trail

♩ = 148

Traditional Cowboy

I'm bound to fol- low the long-horn cows un - til I am too old, It's

well I work for wa- ges boys, I get my pay in gold. My boss - es they all

like me well, they say I'm hard to beat, Be - cause I give 'em a bold stand- off, they

know I've got the cheek.

Yell:
Ki-yi-yipi-yipi-yea

I'm a rowdy cowboy just off the stormy plains,
My trade is girting saddles and pulling bridle reins.
Oh, I can tip the lasso, it is with graceful ease;
I rope a streak of lightining, and ride it where I please. (Yell)

I am a Texas cowboy and I do ride the range;
My trade is cinches and saddles and ropes and bridle reins;
With Stetson hat and jingling spurs and leather up to the knees,
Graybacks as big as chili beans and fighting like hell with fleas.
(Yell)

And if I had a little stake, I soon would married be,
But another week and I must go-the boss said so today.
My girl must cheer up courage and choose some other one,
For I am bound to follow the Lone Star Trail until my race is run.
(Yell)

It almost breaks my heart for to have to go away,
And leave my own little darling, my sweetheart so far away.
But when I'm out on the Lone Star Trail often I'll think of thee,
Of my own dear girl, the darling one, the one I would like to see.
(Yell)

And when I get to a shipping point, I'll get on a little spree,
To drive away the sorrow for the girl that once loved me.
And though red licker stirs us up we'er bound to have our fun,
And I intend to follow the Lone Star Trail until my race is done.
(Yell)

It's when we are on the trail where the dust and bellows fly,
It's fifty miles from water and the grass is scorching-dry;
The boss is mad and ringy as you can plainly see,
And I want to leave the trail and one honest farmer be.
(Yell)

And then there comes a rain, boys, one of the gentle kind;
The lakes git full of water, and the grass is waving fine.
The boss will shed his frown, and a pleasant smile you'll see,
And I want to leave my happly home and a roving cowboy be.
(Yell)

When I got up in Kansas, I had a pleasant dream;
I dreamed I was down on Trinity, down on that pleasant stream;
I dreamt my true love right beside me. she come to go my bail;
I woke up broken-hearted with a yearling by the tail.
(Yell)

143

The Melancholy Cowboy

Cowboy Song

Come all you mel - an - chol - y folks and lis - ten un - to
me, I will sing you a - bout the cow - boy whose hearts so light and
free; He roves all over the prai - rie and at night when he lays
down, His heart's as gay as the flower in May with his bed spread on the
ground. **Yodel** Lee O lay - ee - oo O lee O le - ay hoo O de
doo - doo - doo - doo day - ee Lee O lay - ee - oo O lee
O lee ay - hoo O Lee O lee oo lee ay - ee

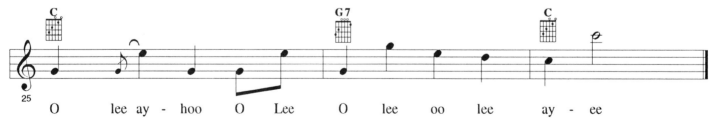

1. Come all you melancholy folks and listen unto me,
I will sing you about the cowboy whose hearts so light and free;
He roves all over the prairie and at night when he lays down,
His heart's as gay as the flowers in May with his bedspread on the ground.

Yodel:
Lee O lay-ee-oo O lee O lee-ay - hoo O de doo-doo-doo-doo day-ee
Lee O lay-ee-oo O lee O lee ay - hoo O lee O lee oo lee ay -ee

2. They're a little rough I must confess the most of them at least,
But as long as you do not cross their trail, You can live with them in place,
But if you do they're sure to rule, the day you come to their land,
For they'll follow you up and shoot it out, they'll do it man to man.
Yodel:

3. You caqn go to a cowboy hungry, go to him wet or dry,
And ask him for a few dollars in change and he will not deny.
He will pull out his pocket book and hand you out a note,
Oh, they are the fellows to strike boys, when ever you are broke.
Yodel:

The Railroad Corral

Happy cowboys getting the steers from range to train, this rousting song was written in 1904 by Joseph Hanson. It was included in the first Lomax collection in 1910.

1. Oh, we're up in the morning ere breaking of day,
The chuck wagon's busy, the flapjacks in play;
The herd is astir o'er hillside and vale,
With the night riders rounding them into the trail.
To Refrain

2. Oh, come take up your cinches, come shake out your reins;
Come wake your old bronco and break for the plains;
come roust out your steers from the long chaparral,
For the outfit is off to the railroad corral.
To Refrain

3. The sun circles upward; the steers as they plod
Are pounding to powder the hot prairie sod;
Now it seems as the dust makes you dizzy and sick
That we'll never reach noon and the cool, shady creek.
To Refrain

4. Now tie up your kerchief and ply up your nag,
Come dry up your grumbles and try not to lag;
Come with your steers from the long chaparral,
For we're far on the road to the railroad corral.
To Refrain

The Range of the Buffalo

Old Cowboy Tune

'Twas in the town of Jacks - bo - ro, in eight - teen eight - y three,—— A
And me not hav - ing an - y job, to Cre - go I did say,—— This
Yes i will pay good wa - ges and the trans - por - ta - tion too,—— Pro

man by name of Cre - go—— came step - ping up to me.—— Says he, "My fine young
job of hunt - ing Buff' - lo—— de - pend up - on the pay,—— But if you pay good
vi - ded you will go with me and stay the sum - mer through,—— But if your blue and

fel - low,—— do you think you'd like to go,—— and spend the sum - mer sea - son—— on the
wag - es,—— and the trans - por - ta - tation too,—— I'd like to spend the sum - er—— on the
home-sick,— and go back to Jacks - bo - ro,—— I won't pay trans - por - ta - tion,—— from the

range of the Buf - fa - lo?——————
range of the Buf - fa - lo?——————
range of the Buf - fa - lo.——————

Verse 4
And now the outfit was complete, nine able bodied men,
In leather chaps and stetson, and Crego, he made ten.
The going out was easy, on the route we had to go,
Until we crossed Peace River, on the range of the Buffalo.

Verse 5
Our daily fare was buffalo with lots of sour-dough bread,
We got so very sick of it, we wished we al were dead,
Th boss he used to haze us 'tho, none of us were slow,
Until we wished we'd never seen, the range of the Buffalo.

Verse 6
But now, we've crossed Peace River, and homeward we are bound,
And in that land forsaken, we'll never more be found,
So back to wives and sweethearts, and tell others not to go,
No matter if they pay your fare, to the range of the Buffalo.

The Song In A Cowboy's Heart

Words and Music by:
Nell Drake Streiffe, Helen L. Ross
and James A. Hime Jr.

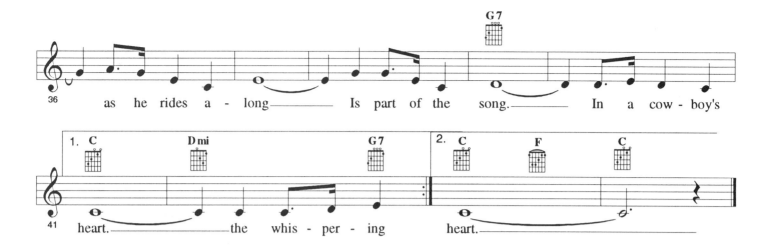

as he rides a - long___ Is part of the song.___ In a cow - boy's

1. C | Dmi | G7 | 2. C | F | C

heart.___the whis - per - ing heart.___

Wilf Carter
Montana Slim

"First of all, let's get back to my boyhood days, what a grand old memory that is. Got my idea about yodeling when about ten years old. I happened to be driving a team of oxen (that was down in Nova Scotia, Canada) some twenty odd years ago, (about 1921). As I was kind of drifting along the trail, I saw a poster with a picture of a fellow called 'The Yodeling Fool'. He was appearing in a show at my home town. After I heard him I sure tried my best at the same line. Yep, got many a paddling at home for many such a noise, but kept practicing when no one was around.

At an early age, I drifted West, riding boxcars from town to town, and finally landed in a town called Calgary, Alberta. What a grand old Cowtown. Got me a job on a ranch as chore boy and as years rolled by, I learned some cowpunchin', followed the Rodeo, and gradually as my yodeling improved, or so folks say, I used to sing around the chuck wagon at round-up time. I later took a crack at trail riding in the mountains but darn it all, I wanted to roam, so hit the trail for New York City. Landed at Columbia Broadcasting Studios and was given a swell job singing good old western tunes. Oh, I've tangled up around two hundred songs or more and get a great kick out of doing it."

Wilf Carter

148

The Tenderfoot

Punching cows for an inexperienced cowboy is all hard work and no play

Old Cowboy Song

One day I thought I'd have some fun and see— just how cow - punch - ing was done and

when the round up had be - gun I tack - led the cat - tle king———— Say

he, "My fore - men went to town He's in a sa - loon and his name is Brown If

you see him he'll take you down." Says I, "that suits me fine."————

We started to the ranch next day,
Brown talked to me most all the way;
Says, "Punching cows is nothing but play,
It is no work at all."
Oh, jim'ny krissmas now he lied,
He sure had a hell of a lot of gall,
He let me manage the cavvy hole,
Says Brown "Don't work too hard.'

They saddled me up an old gray hack,
That had a seat fast on his back;
They padded him down with gunny sack,
And with my bedding too.
When I got on he left the ground,
Wend up in the air and he circled around,
When I came down I busted the ground,
I got a terrible fall.

I've travelled up, I've travelled down,
I've travelled this world all around;
I've lived in city, I've lived in town;
I've got this much to say:
Before you go to punching cows,
Go kiss your wife,
Get insurance on your life,
And shoot yourself with any old knife,
For that is the easiest way.

149

The Texas Rangers

One of the very oldest of cowboy songs this tells of the dangerous life of a Ranger fighting Indians.

Cowboy Song

Come all you Tex - as Ran - gers, where - ev - er you may be, I'll tell you of some trou - bles that hap - ened un - to me. My name is noth - ing ex - tra, so that I will not tell, But here's to all good ran - gers, I'm sure I wish you well.

1. Come all you Texas Rangers, wherever you may be,
I'll tell you of some trouble that happened unto me.
My name is nothing extra, so that I will not tell,
But here's to all good rangers, I'm sure I wish you well.

2. When at the age of sixteen, I joined a jolly band.
We marched from San Antonio down to the Rio Grande.
Our captain he informed us, perhaps he thought it right,
"Before we reach the station, we'll surely have to fight."

3. I saw the smoke ascending, it seemed to reach the sky.
The first thought then came to me, "My time has come to die!"
I thought of my dear mother, in tears to me did say:
"To you they are all strangers, with me you'd better stay."

4. I saw the Indians coming, I heard their awful yell.
My feelings at the moment, no human tongue can tell.
I saw their glittering lances, their arrows around me flew,
Till all my strength had left me and all my courage too.

5. We fought for nine full hours before the strife was o'er.
The likes of dead and dying, I've never seen before.
And when the sun had risen, the Indians they had fled.
We loaded up our rifles and counted up our dead.

The Trail to Mexico

This song was written in 1882 or 1883. It tells of driving cattle from the Texas Panhandle across New Mexico and into Arizona. The long trip results in the cowboy losing his girl.

Lively

The Roaming Ranger

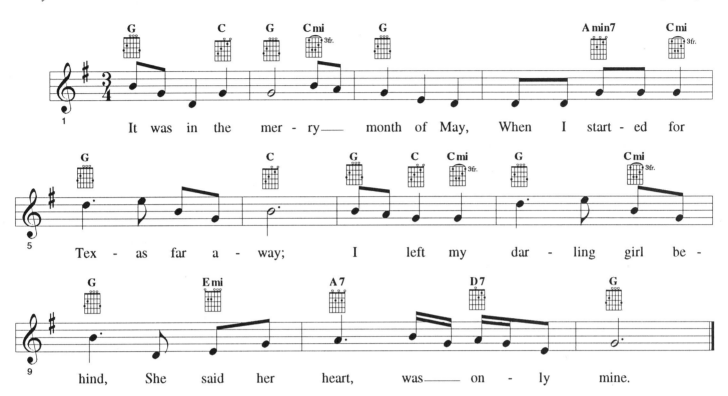

It was in the mer - ry—— month of May, When I start - ed for Tex - as far a - way; I left my dar - ling girl be - hind, She said her heart, was—— on - ly mine.

I made up my mind to mend by way
And quit the crowd that was too gay
To leave my darling girl behind
For she promised me she was only mine.

It was in May merry month of May
When I left for Texas so far away
I left my darling girl behind
she said her heart was mine, all mine.

Oh, when I held her in my arms
I thought she had ten thousand charms
Her caress was soft her kisses sweet;
she said "We'll marry next time we meet.

It was in the year of eighty-three
That A.J. Stinson hired me.
He said, "Young fellow, I want you to go
And drive my cattle to Mexico.

"Twas in the early spring that year
That I took the trail and drove those steers.
With heart so light and a cowboys song
To Mexico we rolled along.

When I got there in Mexico,
I thought of the girl who loved me so,
I wrote a letter then to my dear;
but not one word from her did I hear.

Then I started back to my own loved home
Asked for the girl who was my own
She said, "I've wed a richer life,
So now young fellow get another wife.

Oh curse your gold, and your silver too,
And curse the girl who isn't true;
I'm going back to the Rio Grande
And take a job with a cowboy band."

"Oh buddy, oh buddy, please stay at home
Don't be forever on the roam;
There's many a girl more true than I,
So don't go back where the bullets fly."

"I'm going back where the girls are true;
Where fickle love I never knew
I'm going back where the bullets fly
And stay on the cow trail til I die."

151

The Wandering Cowboy

Tune: "Brown Eyed Lee"
Words by: John R. Craddock

Moderato

I am a wand'ring cowboy, from ranch to ranch I roam.
At ey'ry ranch, when welcome, I make myself at home.
Two years I worked for the Double L and one for the O Bar O,
then drifted west from Texas to the plains of Mexico.

There I met with a rancher who was looking for a hand.
So when springtime greened the valley, I was burning the Bar S brand.
I worked on through the summer then early in the fall,
Over the distant ranges there came the old, old call.

So I drifted to Arizona to work for Uncle Bob,
A-tailing up the weak ones in a winter feeding job.
But the ranch camp grew too lonely, with never a rest or change,
So I saddles up one morning and struck for a distant range.

One night in wild Wyoming when the stars hung bright and low,
I lay in my tarp a-dreaming of the far off home rancho.
When the cottonwood leaves are whisp'ring in the evening soft and low,
"Tis there my heart's a-turning and homeward I must go.

It's now I'm tired of rambling, no longer will I roam,
When my pony I've unsaddled in the old corral at home.
(repeat last two lines)

The Wells and Fargo Line

Cowboy Song

♩ = 148

Lyrics:

Come listen to my story, I'll not detain you long,
A-singing and a-humming this simple silly song.
'Tis of the old ex-convicts, the men who served their time
For robbing mountain stages on the Wells and Fargo line.

There was Major Thompson turned up the other day,
He said that he would hold them up or hell would be to pay,
Or he could hold a rifle and draw a bead so fine
Upon those shotgun messengers of the Wells and Fargo line.

And there was Jimmy Miner who thought he was a thief
But he did surely prove himself to be a dirty sneak;
And now behind San Quentin's walls he's serving out his time
For giving tips to Old Jim Hughes on the Wells and Fargo line.

And there was still another who well did play his part,
He's known among the mountains as the highwayman, Black Bart.
He'd ride those mountain jerkies, to him it was but pleasure,
He'd ride the trail both night and day for the Wells and Fargo treasure.

And now my story's ended, I've not detained you long,
A-singing and a-humming this simple silly song.
And though the nights are long, boys, and weary grows the time,
But when we are out we'll ride again the Wells and Fargo line.

Underlay (verse 1):

Come lis-ten to my sto-ry,—— I'll not de-tain you long, A sing-ing and a hum-ming—— this sim-ple sil-ly song. 'Tis of the old ex-con-victs,—— the men who served their time, For rob-bing moun-tain stag-es on the Wells and Far-go line.——

Trail Boss

Cowboy Tune

Verse

My old Trail Boss, he——— at the age of eight - y three, One

day in May was tak - en ill and died. And——— af - ter he was dead the———

will, of course, was read by a law - yer as we all stood by his side. To my

bro - ther it was told he had left a pouch of gold, the same un - to old cook - ie I de -

clare. but when it came to me, the law-yer said I see he was left to you that sad - dle, there

Chorus:

How they joked, How they teased, How my bro - ther and old cook - ie wheezed when they heard the

law - yer de - clare, the Trail - Boss on - ly left to you that sad - dle there.

My trail-boss, he at the age of eighty-three
One day in May was taken ill and died.
And after he was dead, the will of course was read
By a lawyer as we all stood by his side.
To my brother it was told he had left a pouch of gold
The same unto old cookie, I declare.
But when it came to me, the lawyer said I see
He has left to you that saddle, there.

Chorus:
How they joked, how they teased,
how my brother and old cookie wheezed.
When they heard the lawyer declare,
The Trail-boss only left to you that saddle, there.

I hardly thought it fair, still I said I didn't care
And in the evening took the saddle away.
My brother laughed and said, as he slyly shook his head
You'll find it may be useful, John someday.
When you settle down in life, find a job and get a wife.
You'll find it very handy, I declare.
On a hot and summer night, when the fire-flies are in flight
To be riding in that saddle, there.

Chorus:

What my brother said was true, for in a year or two
Strange to say, I settled down in married life.
At first the girl did court, and then the ring I bought
I took her to the church and then she was my wife.
That dear old girl, and me were as happy as can be
And when it is time to work, I declare
Our cattle ranch I roam
But each day would return home.
And be riding in that saddle, there.

Chorus:

One day the saddle slipped, when I picked it up it ripped
A bag had fallen on the dusty ground.
And there before my eyes, and to my great surprise
Lay ten thousand bills, maybe more that I found.
When my brother heard of this, the fellow, I confess,
Went nearly mad with rage and tore his hair.
But I only looked at him and slyly whispered, Jim,
Don't you wish you had that saddle, there.

Cowboy Tidbits

trail-drives

Also **cattle-drives.** Although herds of cattle could be driven from any one location to another, the classic route for trail-driving was north from Texas. Before the Civil War, there had been a few drives over considerable distances, such as from southwest Texas to Shreveport, Louisiana, and into Mississippi; and also as far north as Sedalia, Missouri, and Quincy, Illinois. Possibly the first recorded long-trailing was done by Edward Piper, from Texas to Ohio, in 1846. But the main Texas trail-driving period was after the war, from 1866 to about 1885. This took cattle to various trail-towns on the railroad that bisected Kansas, on which cows were shipped to the Eastern states. The trail-driving was pushed west, eventually to California, by a quarantine against the Texas cattle and the westward expansion of the railroad. The trails became famous: The Shawnee Trail, the Chisholm Trail, the Western Cattle Trail. Herds were taken as far north as Nebraska, Wyoming, and Montana and were pushed along the lethal stretches of the Southern Trail and up the Goodnight-Loving Trail into Colorado.

The start of such drives was usually made in the spring, so that cattle could feed on the fresh grass as they slowly went north. If the drive was to the northern country, the cattle had to meet the new grazing grounds before the hard winters set it. Spring was also early enough to avoid rivers in flood: at that time most of them were shallow and fordable; a late-started drive could encounter serious trouble at river-crossings.

A herd of steers, without cows or calves along, could maintain a rate of about 15 miles a day, which was the drover's favorite speed: though the driving could be hard at the start, and covered about 20 to 25 miles per day so that the herd could be trail-broke, when it settled down there would be no hurrying, because the cows had to be wellfleshed when they reached their destination. The cattle would be strung out in a long fore-and-aft line and could be drifted along rather than driven. The cook and his wagon would go ahead to look for a spot for noon dinner. The trail-boss would find a good bedding ground for the night. Dinner was around 11:00 in the morning so the cattle could graze through noon. Ideally, a herd was well-fed and watered before they were settled down for the night.

 A herd of 3,000 would need something like 10 to 15 drovers, one of whom would be the foreman, or trail-boss who was appointed by the owner or owners and was usually, at least in later years, an experienced professional who had made several such drives. How he gathered his herd depended upon time and place. During the early days in Texas he or his employer would gather all the cattle on a range and road-brand them, taking careful note of all the brands gathered so that the owners could be reimbursed when the entire herd had been sold in Kansas.

The cook was one of the most important men on the drive: he had to be good or the crew would be bad. The men were hired in pairs so that two-man watches could be made up. A hand's status could be seen from his position on the drive. First came the pointers at the head of the herd, then the swing, followed by the flankers. In the rear was the drag. Among some trail-crews, some men might change positions, but usually the pointers kept their posts for the entire drive. The pay for all hands was generally somewhat better than that of a cowboy on the range, and the cook received a higher wage than the ordinary drover.

In the best outfits, each hand would have a string or mount of eight to ten horses (the boss, who rode farther and harder than any other member of the crew, would have a few more). He would need every one of them and had to know each of them well. With a number of rivers to cross, each man preferred to have at least one good swimming horse and one to use for a hard run. He also had what he called his "night horse," one that was sure-footed and confident in the dark. The choosing of these horses was an important occasion: probably lots would be drawn for the first choice; after that the men could choose freely. And God help the man who helped himself to another man's horse. The horse-herd was in the charge of the wrangler or remudero, usually a young and comparatively inexperienced hand. He had to know every horse in his band and to which hand it belonged, and was expected to be able to rope whichever one was called for at any time of day or night. When he slept is a matter for puzzlement.

To give some idea of the number of cattle that went up the trail into Kansas from Texas, in 1866, the first year of the big drives something like 260,000 head went north. The total fluctuated from year to year, but in 1871, the all-time high of about 600,000 was reached. As late as 1885, 350,000 went north.

Texas abounded not only in cattle but in horses and burros. Large herds of both are well recorded. Texas cowponies were in great demand in Wyoming and Montana, and it was said that in 1884 some 100,000 were exported from Texas; throughout the range period a total of one million went to supply the needs of the cattle industry. Burros were driven in vast herds to the mines of Colorado. Both turkeys and razorbacks found themselves driven in herds over the long trails by intrepid Texans.

waddy

Originally thought to be a temporary hand taken on at round-up, to wad out the normal outfit. Several authorities state that the term was originally applied to a cow-thief, but later was used to cover all cowhands. It has been suggested that it originated from chewing a wad of tobacco.

wallet

(Texas) A saddle sack. A wallet is a sack with both ends sewed up and a hole in the middle to put things in, half on one side of the hole and half on the other.

Trail Dust

Moderato

Words and Music by:
W. Spencer Nale, Fern DeSavis
and Morris Scrogin

There's dust a-ris-in' on the West-ern hor-i-zon, Are the do-gies on the roam? Where the herd is mill-in' and the dust is spill-in' Are the rid-ers head-in' home? Trail Dust ris-in' in the blue, Where are the rid-ers head-in' to? Are the do-gies there in dan-ger, is it on-ly some strang-ers rid-in' through? Trail Dust on the set-tin' sun, Has the round-up just be-gun? Are the buf-flo' on the wan-der, is the herd o-ver yon-der on the run? To-night when the dust has fall-en and the moon's o'er the chap-ar-

al, To - night while the des - erts' call - in' will we meet at the old cor -

ral? Trail Dust trail - in' up a bove, Drift - in' on the boots and

glove, Is the round - up all in or - der, is he com - in' 'cross the bor - der, Are you

send - in' back my love? love?

Even cowboys drink a
Coca-Cola **now and then c. 1941**

When the Campfire is Low on the Prairie

Music and Lyrics by:
Sam H. Stept

When the moon's o - ver head and the worlds' gone to bed,

I find con - tent - ment each night, By a camp - fire, my

dreams come to life and it seems they make ev - 'ry - thing come out

right. When the camp - fire is low on the

prai - rie, And my brand - in' is done for the day,

Then I sit by the fire on the prai - rie And I

dream of my love far a - way, When I talk to my

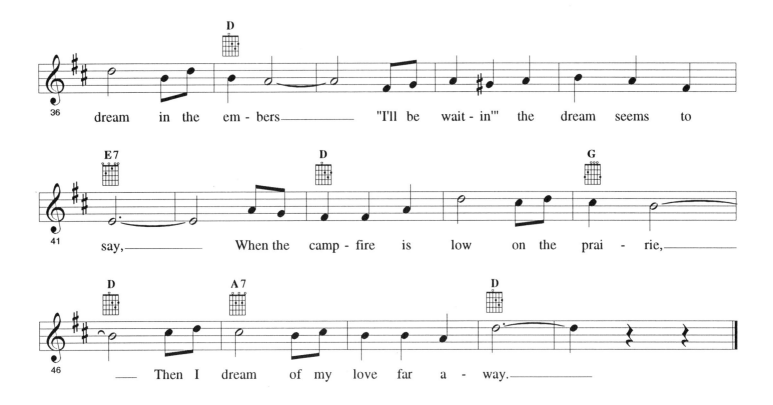

dream in the em - bers_____ "I'll be wait - in'" the dream seems to say,_____ When the camp - fire is low on the prai - rie,_____ _____ Then I dream of my love far a - way._____

When the Campfire is Low on the Prairie, these Montana buckaroos are ready to hit the trail with their bed rolls piled high on this wagon, there's even a spare saddle on top. c. 1910.

When the Prairie Campfires Burn

Old Cowboy Tune

When the Prai - rie Camp - fires Burn, to guide our safe re - turn, We'll
head our wear - y pon - ies glad - ly home,——— When the prai - rie breez - es sigh, a
west - ern lul - la - by, We'll blank - et 'neath the stars of heav - en's dome.——— And we'll
won - der if 'way up there, in ans - wer to their prayer, They're round - in' up the dog - ies in the
sky,——— When the Prai - rie Camp - fires Burn, Be - neath the stars we yearn to
find that cow - boy's heav - en by and by.———

When the Wind Blows Out In Plainville

(Comedy Song)

Words and Music by:
Henry A. Bundy, Nora I. Baldwin and J. Dobbs

When the wind blows out in Plain-ville it sweeps the prai-rie clean, the sand-hills fly, the cows go dry and riv-ers run up-stream, When the wind blows out in Plain-ville they change the map each day, towns move a-round and once they found Dodge Cit-y in San-ta Fe; It's a great life in Plain-ville, where balm-y breez-es blow, It's a great life in Plain-ville, where things are on the go. 2. When the say.

When the folks 'way out in Plainville are hangin' in the trees,
They never mind, it's just a kind of playful western breeze.
Uncle Ned had forty acres he planted in the sky,
That Uncle Joe in Idaho will harvest bye an' bye;
It's a great life in Plainville, don't weaken when you say
It's a great life in Plainville, where the wind blows ev'ry day.

Cousin Lou from Kansas City blew by one windy day,
"Hello, farewell", they heard her yell, "I'm sorry I can't stay,"
When you've lost your home an' cattle an' they're sailin' o'er the hills
Just smile and say, "Oh that's okay, the government pays the bills;"
It's a great life in Plainville, where prairie breezes play,
It's a great life in Plainville, if you don't care what you say.

Wild Buckaroo

A bragging cowboy tells of his wild buckaroo lifestyle

Cowboy Song

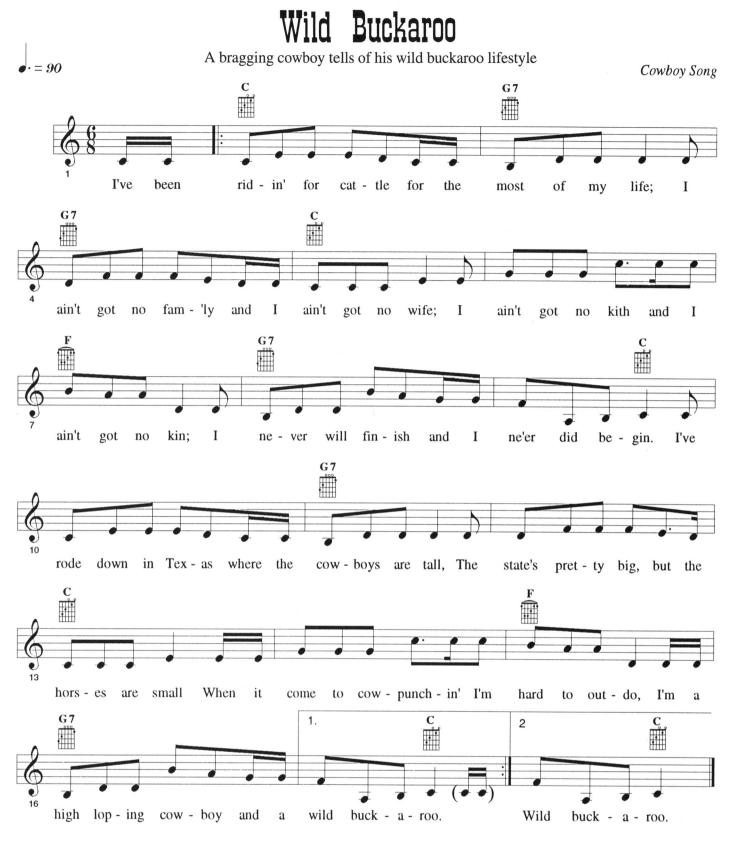

I've been ridin' for cattle for the most of my life; I ain't got no fam-'ly and I ain't got no wife; I ain't got no kith and I ain't got no kin; I ne-ver will fin-ish and I ne'er did be-gin. I've rode down in Tex-as where the cow-boys are tall, The state's pret-ty big, but the hors-es are small When it come to cow-punch-in' I'm hard to out-do, I'm a high lop-ing cow-boy and a wild buck-a-roo. Wild buck-a-roo.

I've been ridin' for cattle for the most of my life;
I ain't got no family and I ain't got no wife;
I ain't got no kith and I ain't got no kin;
I never will finish and I ne'er did begin.
I've rode down to Texas where the cowboys are tall,
The state's pretty big, but the horses are small.
When it comes to cowpunchin' I'm hard to out-do -
I'm a high-loping cowboy and a wild buckaroo.

I have rode up in Montana and I've rode in Idaho,
I have rode for old Terasus down in old Mexico.
I have roped a mountain lion and a she grizzly bear;
I have used a choya cactus fer to comb my hair.
I have rode across the desert with the water far between,
And I've crossed Death Valley without a canteen.
When it comes to crossin' deserts, I'm hard to out-do -
I'm a high-loping cowboy and a wild buckaroo.

I talk a lot of Spanish and I talk Piute,
Oh, I pack a long knife and a pistol to shoot.
I got no *senorita,* and I got no squaw,
I got no sweetheart nor no mother-in-law.
I have never been tied to no apron strings,
Oh,. I ain't no devil, but I got no wings.
When it comes to dodgin' women, I'm had to out-do -
I'm a high-loping cowboy and a wild buckaroo.

Oh, I don't like whiskey, but I do like my beer.
Oh, I don't like mutton, but I do like steer.
I will let you alone if you'll let me be,
But don't you think you can crawl on me.
I will fight anybody at the drop of a hat
And he'll think he's in a sack with a panther cat.
When it comes to whipping bad men, I'm hard to out-do -
I'm a high-loping cowboy and a wild buckaroo.

You'll Like What You Hear!

Guitar books from Centerstream Publishing
P.O. Box 17878 - Anaheim Hills, CA 92807   (714) - 779-9390

Guitar Chords Plus
by Ron Middlebrook
Centerstream Publishing
A comprehensive study of normal and extended chords, tuning, keys, transposing, capo, and more. Includes lots of helpful photos and diagrams, a key to guitar symbols, and a glossary of guitar terms.
00000011 ....$11.95

Blues Guitar Legends
by Kenny Sultan
Centerstream Publishing
This book/CD package allows you to explore the styles of Lightnin' Hopkins, Blind Blake, Mississippi John Hurt, Blind Boy Fuller, and Big Bill Broonzy. Through Sultan's arrangements, you will learn how studying the masters can help you develop your own style.
_____00000181 Book/CD Pack $19.95

Flying Fingers*
by Dave Celentano
Centerstream Publications
Your fingers will be flying over the guitar neck as this book/cassette demonstrates proven techniques that increase speed, precision and dexterity. 32 examples cover alternate picking, sweep picking and circular picking. Cassette demonstrates techniques at three speeds: slow, medium and fast.
_____00000103 Book/Cassette Pack.............$15.95

Survival Licks & Bar Room Tricks*
by Mark & J.R.
Centerstream Publications
A survival guide for today's music scene – from learning how to solo in a variety of styles to how to protect yourself from flying bottles. After reading this book, you will be equipped with the knowledge and confidence it takes to pull any gig off. Includes country, blues, rock, metal and jazz fusion licks in notes and tab.
_____00000133 ....$8.95

Over The Top
by Dave Celentano
Centerstream Publications
A new book/CD pack by Dave Celentano for guitarists who want to concentrate on their 2-hand tapping tech-nique.

_____00000166 Book/CD Pack......................$17.95

Pedal Steel Licks For Guitar*
by Forest Rodgers
Centerstream Publishing
Learn to play 30 popular pedal steel licks on the guitar. All 30 examples are played three times on the accompanying CD. Also features tips for the best steel guitar sound reproduction, and steel guitar voiced chords.
_____00000183 Book/CD Pack $15.95

SCALES AND MODES IN THE BEGINNING
by Ron Middlebrook
Centerstream Publications
The most comprehensive and complete scale book written especially for the guitar. Divided into four main sections: 1) Fretboard Visualization, the breaking down of the whole into parts; 2) Scale Terminology – a thorough understanding of whole and half steps, scale degrees, intervals, etc.; 3) Scales And Modes – the rear of the book covers every scale you will ever need with exercises and applications; 4) Scale To Chord Guide – ties it all together, showing what scale to use over various chords.
_____00000010...........................$11.95

Modal Jams And Theory
Using The Modes For Solo Guitar
by Dave Celentano
Centerstream Publications
Not only will this book show you how to play the modes, it will also show you the theory behind mode construction, how to play any mode in any key, how to play the proper mode over a given chord progression, and how to write chord progressions for each of the seven modes. The accompanying CD includes two rhythm tracks (drums, bass, keyboard and rhythm guitar), and a short solo for each mode so guitarists can practice their solos with a "real" band.
_____00000163 Book/CD Pack....................$17.95

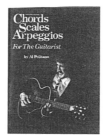

The Complete Book Of Chords, Scales, Arpeggios For The Guitar*
by Al Politano
Centerstream Publications
Every chord, scale and arpeggio is plotted out in every practical position and with some dedicated study, one could play all of them in every position and in all keys. Written with just a minimum amount of verbalization. Use this book for improvisation, studying or playing exercises. This is the best, most complete reference book you can buy.
_____00000021 ....$8.95

Electric Blues Guitar
by Derek Cornett
Centerstream Publications
An introduction to the most commonly used scales and techniques for the modern blues player, complete with CD. Includes musical examples to show how scales are used in improvisation, and play-along tunes that provide a "hands-on" start to improvisation.
_____00000165 Book/CD Pack........................$17.95

POWER RHYTHM GUITAR
by Ron Middlebrook with Dave Celentano
Centerstream Publications
This book/CD pack features 31 lessons for rhythm guitar that you can play by yourself, in a band, or as a back-up musician. Includes full band examples in many musical styles, including basic rock, country, hard rock, heavy metal, reggae, blues, funk, and more.
_____00000113 Book/CD Pack...................$17.95

Guitar Tuning For The Complete Idiot (For Smart People Too)*
Centerstream Publications
By Ron Middlebrook
A complete book on how to tune up. Tuning record included. Contents include: Everything You Need To Know About Tuning – with several methods explained; Intonation – what it is and how to set your guitar up; Strings – How To Find The Right Ones For You; 12 String Tuning; Picks; and much more.
_____00000002 ....$5.95

Open Guitar Tunings*
Centerstream Publications
The only book that illustrates over 75 different tunings in easy-to-read diagrams. Includes tunings used by artists such as Chet Atkins, Michael Hedges, Jimmy Page, Joe Satriani and more for rock, blues, bluegrass, folk and country styles including open D (for slide guitar), Em, open C, modal tunings and many more.
_____ 00000130 ....$4.95

P.O. Box 17878 - Anaheim Hills, CA 92807   (714) - 779-9390

"How The West Was Sung"
Western Music Books
from CENTERSTREAM Publications
P. O. Box 17878 Anaheim Hills, CA 92807
Phone/Fax (714) 779-9390 - E-Mail, Centerstrm @ AOL.com

How to Yodel "The Cowboy Way"
by Rudy Robbins & Shirley Field
Centerstream Publishing
This book/CD pack by Rudy Robbins, of the official Texan cowboy band Spirit of Texas, and Shirley Field, Canada's champion female yodeler, will teach you how to yodel in no time! Features basic instructions, simple songs, recorded demonstrations, and a special photo gallery & short bios of cowboy and cowgirl yodelers.
00000207 Book/CD Pack $19.95

Ranger Doug – Songs of the Sage, No. 1
foreword by Texas Bix Bender
Centerstream Publishing
Features original western songs from Ranger Doug Green, the idol of American youth and member of the popular western singing group Riders In The Sky. Includes 25 songs from their many recordings: Blue Montana Skies • Night Riding Song • Here Comes The Santa Fe • That's How The Yodel Was Born • Lonely Yukon Stars • Prairie Serenade • and many more. Features the story behind each song, plus lots of photos. "It's the cowboy way!"
00000206 ....$15.95

SONGS 'ROUND THE CAMPFIRE
compiled by Ron Middlebrook
Centerstream Publications
96 of your favorite songs sung by "Hi" Busse, Tom Chambers, Robert Meyer, Dan Meyer, Tom Spaulding, Bob Wagoner, Buck Page, John Ryberg, John Lamount, Tex Ritter, and Carson Robinson. Also includes old cowboy photographs, a glossary of cowboy terms, bios of songwriters, Tumbleweed History, and more.
00000037..$24.95

Songs Of The Cowboy
compiled by Ron Middlebrook
Centerstream Publications
This unique collection celebrates the romance attached to the cowboy and his free-roaming lifestyle. By combining classic cowboy songs, trivia, photos, articles and diagrams with current cowboy songwriters' songs, this book pays special tribute to our Western musical heritage. ♪

$12.95 • 9x12 • 96 pages • Softcover • 0-931759-46-3 • HL00000129

SINGING THE STORIES OF THE WEST
Book/CD Pack
by Ernie Sites
Centerstream Publishing
Contains great songs of the New and Old West in melody line/lyrics/guitar chord arrangements, poems, photos & illustrations, and fascinating facts and the background history of the West. Songs include: Whoopee Ki-Yi-Yo (Git Along Little Dogies) • The Old Chisholm Trail • Carry Me Back To The Lone Prairie • Home On The Range • Bad Brahma Bull • I'm Just A Little Cowpoke • more. CD includes Ernie Sites singing the songs and reciting the poems.
_____00000198 Melody/Lyrics/Chords........$14.95

Songs Of The Trail
compiled by Ron Middlebrook
foreword by Rusty Richards
Centerstream Publications
Cowboys have always held a special place in the hearts and imaginations of Americans. Images of riding bravely and happily into the sunset, fending off dangerous enemies, and singing around the campfire evoke a sense of pride and respect for a lifestyle nearly forgotten in this age of progress. Relive the days of the cowboys bringing the herds home in this interesting compilation of facts and music. 53 songs celebrate the life and times on the range by such noted writers as Doc Denning, Chris LeDoux, Rusty Richards, Roy Rodgers Jr., and others. Their music is an actual view into their daily adventures, tribulations and entertainment. This unique publication also features articles on black cowboys, cowgirls, cowboys' Spanish ancestry, and more. ♪

$14.95 • 9x12 • 112 pages • Softcover • 0-931759-67-6 • HL00000152